Gimme Shelter

a life of public service in New York City

BONNIE STONE

Enjoy the book!

BROOKLYN
RIVER
PRESS

Gimme Shelter

a life of public service in New York City

Bonnie Stone

Enjoy the book!

BROOKLYN
RIVER
PRESS

Published in the United States by
Brooklyn River Press
New York

ISBN 978-0-9882675-4-1

Book designed by Ken Feisel

In memory of

My loving parents, SAU AND MIKE

and

My work husband, HY BURTON,
who stood by me for 15 years

CONTENTS

PROLOGUE

I KNOCKED ON A DOOR at the end of a dimly lit corridor. After a few seconds, I heard a sequence of locks and deadbolts click before the door opened a crack, still restrained by the chain inside. A small pair of frightened eyes peered out. I explained to the elderly woman behind the door that I was part of a research project studying the experience and perception of crime in two New York City Housing Authority projects in Brooklyn. If she was okay with it, I wanted to ask her a series of questions. She agreed and, after answering a few, revealed how trapped she felt inside her apartment because she was terrified of all the crime happening right outside her door. She admitted she couldn't even throw her garbage away down the hall without fearing she'd be attacked, and said that the next time she encountered a mugger she was going to fight back and beat them with her cane.

"Don't do that!" I said. "They'll kill you."

"That's exactly what I want them to do."

By 1970, I was well schooled in research, statistics, and analysis. I had a master's in psychological measurement from Columbia and another in urban planning from New York University. I'd received a scholarship that required me to work part-time, so I'd joined this research team led by the renowned architect Oscar Newman, studying crime patterns in city Housing Authority projects. The conclusions of our team's research became *Defensible Spaces*, now a classic text in urban planning.

Encompassing 177,000 apartments and more than 400,000 residents, the Housing Authority is a vital part of New York City. Most projects are bleak, unappealing buildings, usually set back and separate from the street in a dull, scruffy landscape. Knocking on those apartment doors was, for me, the start of a journey. Interviewing people in the projects, I encountered what was for me an unknown world of suffering, and I learned about the painful effects of poverty and crime up close and personal. My encounter with the old woman peering from behind a door that was her only protection from a brutally violent world was an intense and terribly traumatic experience for me. Her pain was more than I could handle, and the only way I could manage my feelings was to shove them deep inside and maintain a "tough guy" exterior. Conducting interviews, I cultivated a self-serving and probably psychotic delusion that all these people were actors hired to answer their doors for me . . . just so that I could do my job.

Researchers were always accompanied by a police escort, and one day my escort's radio sounded an alert—an armed robbery was in progress right outside, and the escort dashed off and commandeered a bakery truck to pursue the thief. I was surprised to find that not only was I not scared, but I found the chasing-the-bad-guys part thrilling. Then and there I realized how much I wanted to be part of this world; not as a cop but as a different kind of protector, a person who could make lasting changes in other people's lives. So I decided to work for the City of New York.

On August 9, 1945, the same day the United States dropped an atomic bomb on Nagasaki, Japan, I was born in Brooklyn, New York, to a large, loving, and very Jewish family. We lived in a small two-family house with no locks on any of the doors in the Midwood section of Brooklyn. My parents, Sau and Mike, didn't have much money, but in our house, love reigned supreme. I had two older brothers: Lewis, who was 7½ years older than me, and David, who was older by just 3½ years. I was an exuberant, energetic child and, later on, a tomboy and a bit of a tough guy. My brothers and I understood our job: go to school and behave—though behaving wasn't necessarily top of the list. We were of course expected to go to college, because that's just what you did.

James Madison High School, the large public school I attended, was an incubator for bright students because the education was superb. Over the years, Madison produced numerous accomplished people, including Supreme Court Justice Ruth Bader Ginsburg, who graduated 12 years before me; Senator Bernie Sanders, who was just 4 years ahead of me; and Senator Chuck Schumer, who followed me by 6 years. Graduates of James Madison include six Nobel Prize recipients, a Minnesota senator, singer-songwriter Carole King, and Judge Judy of television fame. There was even a famous athlete, Rudy LaRusso, a six-foot, eight-inch basketball forward who played for the LA Lakers.

I enjoyed school and loved science until the summer before my senior year. That summer I went to an eight-week program in Bridgeport, Connecticut, for aspiring scientists, sponsored by the National Science Foundation. I'd received a scholarship to study biology for nearly a whole summer, and I was completely excited. But there was a professor in charge of my group who always picked out two kids to humiliate and scapegoat, and even though he never did anything to me, I became hysterical just observing his meanness. By the end of the first week, I couldn't stand it anymore and phoned my parents, tearfully demanding to come home. They were stunned. They said I'd get over it, but I didn't, and a couple of days later I called them again and they came and got me. I was at home sitting on the couch with my mother, expecting her to be supportive, since she always was.

"Why did you have to leave?" she asked.

"Because he was horrible!"

"Well . . . ?"

I got the message. That he was horrible was not a good enough reason to give up on the program.

"Do you think I should go back?"

"Yes, I do."

I was confounded, but I did go back. Still, I'd lost all my initial exuberance and excitement about the program. I told the dean about the mean professor, but it didn't change a thing, because he was still there and nothing happened to him. Then I kept very quiet. I commiserated with a few other kids I liked but kept my head down. The experience frightened me and, unfortunately, turned me off of science forever. I figured, *Well, if this is science, I don't want any part of it, even if I'm good at it.* I came home at the end of the summer convinced I'd flunk out of high school.

At that time, Madison allowed its senior students to apply to only four colleges, so I went for broke and applied to four Ivy League colleges with no "safe" option. I was rejected by Wellesley but wait-listed by Radcliffe, the University of Pennsylvania, and Cornell. The Wellesley rejection was no surprise. Earlier that year my beloved English teacher, Debbie Tannenbaum, overheard a harshly worded telephone conversation between our assistant principal, Ms. Horne, and the Wellesley recruiter. Ms. Horne described me as a difficult and troublesome student. I was shocked when I heard this. In my years at James Madison, I had never even talked to Ms. Horne, much less given her any reason to have such a strong negative impression of me. My father wanted to confront her, but my mother talked him out of it. In 1961, one did not easily question authority.

Two years later, while I was home for winter break, an old friend visited me in Brooklyn. She said she'd heard that Ms. Horne had confused me with Betty Stone, another student who'd apparently had some dealings with Ms. Horne. A case of mistaken identity had wrecked my chances with the Ivy League.

Back in '61, though, with my college freshman year looming and no firm acceptance in hand, we called the Radcliffe admissions office, and they assured me I'd be admitted from the waiting list. But this was the era when the baby boomers began to hit college age, and none of the schools I applied to accessed their waiting lists that year.

In my neighborhood, not getting into college was every high school graduate's nightmare. I didn't know enough to panic, but I did scramble hard and found out from a classmate that the University of Wisconsin was still accepting out-of-state applications and that it was a "good enough" school. I applied to Wisconsin and was accepted.

In September 1962, my mother wanted to make the trip to the Midwest with me. Since she was afraid of flying, we took a sleeping compartment on the famous 20th Century Limited from Grand

Central Station to Chicago. It was a great adventure for both of us. I was really wound up, and we hardly slept a wink. After we checked into our hotel room in Chicago, we decided to do some sightseeing and wound up at the Art Institute of Chicago late in the afternoon. After we'd taken in several of the exhibits, the museum lights began to dim, indicating that it was closing. More and more rooms went dark as we wended our way through a few more exhibits trying to find an exit, because if we didn't find one a.s.a.p., we'd be locked in the museum overnight! We ran through a large storage area filled with statues draped in thick plastic sheets and covered with plaster dust. We kept running, finally escaped through an obscure exit, and laughed all the way back to the hotel. The next morning, we boarded another train for the three-hour journey to Madison.

The dorm to which I had been assigned was an old mansion on Lake Mendota that had been converted to a private dormitory that could accommodate 50 girls. There were 25 double rooms, common bathrooms, living and dining areas, and a full-time housemother and cook. It was like a friendly sorority house without the rituals. My mother was allowed to stay in my dorm overnight before beginning her journey back home. We said a wistful goodbye the following morning, and I began trying to settle in to dorm life. I quickly made friends with my roommate, Lynn, from Nashville, and soon discovered that almost all the other girls were from out of state too.

I met fellow New Yorker Elizabeth Lambert, and she and I bonded quickly and forever. During college, Elizabeth and I lived on the wild side and must have dated at least 100 different guys. Senior year, we bought a 15-year-old turquoise jalopy off a local farmer for $35. To anyone else, it was a total piece of junk. You could see the road through the floorboards, and the rear door was held closed by a piece of rope. But to us, it might as well have been a Porsche! Elizabeth became a serious abstract painter, and we remained close until her death in 2015.

The University of Wisconsin, with its enrollment of 24,000 students, was huge, diverse, and tons of fun. It was the beginning of the era of sex, drugs, and rock and roll, and the campus was a hotbed of anti–Vietnam War protests and civil rights demonstrations.

I met people from all over, excelled in my classes, and began to grow up. When I graduated in June 1966 with a major in psychology, I had not given a thought to my future. Other students had thought seriously about their life plans—graduate degrees, marriage, family, etc.—but I had no such thoughts. BA from the University of Wisconsin in hand, I didn't have a clue.

Just before graduation, an assistant professor I'd met while doing part-time lab work asked me if I'd be interested in a three-year, all-expenses-paid fellowship in educational psychology there at Madison. I knew nothing about educational psychology but asked how to apply. The professor said I wouldn't have to write an application or compete for the fellowship in any way; all I had to do was say I wanted it, and it was mine. In those years, National Defense Education Act money flowed like water. The federal government was giving graduate scholarships to just about everyone, and this fellowship was very generous, so I accepted it. It would enable me, at no cost, to spend three more years in Madison, a town I'd grown to love. I went back to New York and spent that summer with family and friends before returning for graduate school that September.

When I returned to Madison, my life changed dramatically. I began an illicit affair with a married professor I'd met by chance back in June, a nuclear physicist born in Italy, whose Jewish family had fled Italy during the war. He'd been raised in São Paulo, Brazil, had been educated at Cambridge, and was now a professor of physics at the University of Wisconsin. He was handsome and exotic, and 20 years my senior. What began as just a lark for me soon developed into a passionate love affair. But after a while, the affair turned torturous, and I knew I had to leave Madison. I returned my fellowship with the lame excuse that I needed to take care of family matters back East, and after arranging to attend graduate school at Columbia University, I returned to New York.

I lived in a sprawling apartment on West 110th Street near Columbia University with my former classmates from Wisconsin. Those were extremely unsettled times; the Vietnam War was raging, and antiwar demonstrations were growing louder and more forceful as the government's attempts to squelch them became more severe.

Antiwar activists blew up the mathematics building at the University of Wisconsin, killing a graduate student. A campus takeover at Columbia in 1968 culminated in the police storming the campus. National Guard troops opened fire at a demonstration on the campus of Kent State University, killing four students and severely wounding nine others. The '60s had begun with a great sense of hope for a new generation as John F. Kennedy became the youngest elected president, but after his assassination in November 1963, the country took a dark turn. The war escalated and thousands of US soldiers died. The horror of the war was on television every night, and by 1968, tensions over it and the civil rights movement were tearing the country apart. Then Martin Luther King Jr. and Bobby Kennedy were assassinated, and Richard Nixon was elected president.

I was not your stereotypical "flower power" hippie. I was not a leader of a protest movement, nor would I have called myself an activist. But the political and cultural climate did have a profound influence on me. I was vehemently antiwar, and when I thought about my future, could not imagine joining the corporate world, slipping into the dreaded "establishment," or even academia. In 1968, with my master's almost complete, I applied for a job working with the United States Coast Guard on Governors Island. It was a strange match for an antiwar zealot, for sure, but everybody knew the Coast Guard was a way for draftees to avoid Vietnam War service. Commander Susie Turner interviewed me and offered me a job, and I became a civilian employee of the US Coast Guard with a fairly high GS-11 federal civil service ranking.

So, there I was, a 23-year-old antiwar pothead who looked even younger, supervising seven middle-aged warrant officers. Our task was to create promotion tests for various occupational specialties: aviation, electronics, mechanics, boatswains, food service, gunners, yeomen, intelligence. Commander Turner had hired me because she was afraid a civilian man might be hard pressed to relate to these hard-bitten career warrant officers. She figured I might be such a novelty that the officers would accept me, and they did.

Because Vietnam was an undeclared war, the Coast Guard was prohibited from taking part, and any potential draftee could sign up for the Coast Guard as an alternative to the army. Had the United States officially declared war, the Coast Guard would have become part of the US Navy and would have taken an active role in the military campaign. However, without an official declaration, the Coast Guard was able to maintain its many peacetime duties in the nation's ports and weather stations. There was tension between two groups in the Coast Guard that caused a strained atmosphere. Most enlisted men were happy to have avoided the war, whereas many of the officers were frustrated at being kept out of the action. They wanted combat experience, while the men they commanded just wanted to smoke dope, do their time, and stay alive.

I got along well with Coast Guard people from all over the United States. I lunched on a New York Harbor tugboat, visited lighthouses on the East Coast, and just generally thrived. When a new captain was installed as the head of the training center, I persuaded him to join me at a "be-in" in Central Park. He donned his civvies, and off we went. But when we reached the park, he panicked. "I can't stay. I have to go," he said. That's how uncomfortable he was just being near a "countercultural" event. At least I tried. . . .

After I'd worked with the Coast Guard for a year, a senior congressman from Oklahoma City demanded jobs for his district, and the Johnson administration moved the Coast Guard training center from New York to Oklahoma City. From Oklahoma City it was 1,500 miles to the nearest ocean; a peculiar location for the Coast Guard, indeed. But the decision was political, not logical, so the training center bade farewell to New York Harbor and headed for the prairie. My colleagues tried to convince me to move to Oklahoma City with them, but that was a nonstarter for me. I agreed to fly down for a few days to check it out; saw a few sights, bought a cowboy hat. But in no time I was back on the plane to New York.

After the Coast Guard, I worked with a small consulting firm that conducted employee attitude surveys. I went to Connecticut to interview employees in a tire manufacturing company and to Virginia to speak to people working in tobacco cigarette factories. I interviewed Merrill Lynch employees in upstate New York. I also scored licensing tests for the National Association of Security Dealers. Overall, these jobs were deadly boring, and when they laid me off for lack of work, I was thrilled. I qualified for unemployment *and* I could go back to school, reroute, and hopefully change careers. I enrolled in New York University Graduate School for Public Administration, where I received a master's degree in urban planning and found a part-time research job that introduced me to another world.

Throughout my career, people often asked what I had studied in school in order to do all these unusual jobs. I'd tell them about my two degrees, one in psychological measurement and one in urban planning, and that seemed to suffice as an answer. But the truth was altogether different. Yes, my graduate education gave me technical skills, particularly in statistics, but I never studied social work or political science. I had a liberal arts degree, but most of my graduate education was technical. Not only my career but my whole consciousness evolved as I worked for the government of the city of New York. I was a quick study and extremely fortunate to receive plenty of on-the-job training and wisdom from excellent supervisors. In the process, I was tenacious, some would say obsessed, with what I did. And I was nearly fearless. The downside was that I was missing a reverse gear—something to slow me down a bit and help me know when to relinquish something, when to step gracefully away. I enjoyed crashing through barriers and obstacles, first by really understanding them, then by figuring my way out of, through, over, or around them. My greatest gift was that I got along well with all sorts of people—other bureaucrats, addicts, politicians of any stripe, as well as grassroots community folk. I maintained a strategic, somewhat tough-guy image so that sometimes I intimidated people. But I rarely made enemies.

My oldest brother, Lewis, had been an assistant counsel to New York governor Nelson Rockefeller for several years and knew a lot of government people. Lewis opened the door for me to interview with Jerry Kretschmer, the city's administrator of Environmental Protection, which at that time included the Sanitation Department. Kretschmer had just filled several entry-level management analyst positions, but he sent my résumé to the Health Department. I was called in for an interview but was not much impressed with the desk job they offered in the personnel department. I wanted a job in the field, so I kept on working with the research group.

A year later, I interviewed again with the Health Department, and this time they had an opening in the city's controversial Methadone Maintenance Treatment Program (MMTP). It seemed like a promising opportunity, and I took the job.

Taking that job launched my career. At the time, I hardly knew it would be the beginning of a kaleidoscope odyssey in city and state government that I look back on now as the most fascinating and rewarding time in my life. I didn't know that entering public service was like taking a vow, and that my life would be service, service, service 24 hours a day, seven days a week for the next 18 years.

CHAPTER 1

METHADONIA

A MIDDLE-AGED AFRICAN AMERICAN WOMAN stared out at me from a poster hanging on the wall of the Franklin Street subway station. She had a sparkle in her eye and a warm, inviting smile. Above her photo, it read, *I'm living proof that methadone treatment works.* The poster was part of the New York City Health Department's $4.3 million public education campaign launched in November 2017, in response to a new, widespread epidemic of opioid abuse and related deaths. The Living Proof campaign was created to raise public awareness of the availability of methadone for opioid addiction.

Methadone was no stranger to New York City, even though most New Yorkers were unaware that 44,000 of their fellow citizens were already in methadone treatment when the Living Proof campaign began. Methadone treatment for opioid addiction has been available in New York since the 1970s, when the city began to offer methadone for New Yorkers struggling with substance abuse during a massive epidemic. The treatment was highly controversial, but in the early '70s, Mayor John Lindsay's health administrator, Gordon Chase, and a little-known physician by the name of Dr. Robert Newman weathered the criticism and made lifesaving methadone maintenance available to tens of thousands of heroin addicts. Working with them was my first job in city government. It was a job many would have shunned, detesting city government, methadone, *and* heroin addicts.

Mind-altering substances have been part of human culture since before recorded time. Archaeologists examining human remains trace a long history of mind-altering substance use back to at least 4000 BC. Ancient texts from the Bible to the Babylonian Talmud to Homer's *Odyssey* and the writings of Aristotle have described the use of psychoactive substances and even issued warnings about the dangers of their overuse. Opioids are a class of drugs derived from the seed of the poppy flower and are often used to relieve acute or chronic pain. Opium, the oldest opioid, can be traced back to the ancient Sumerians in what is present-day Iraq. From Sumeria, opium spread across Europe and Asia following trade and migration routes so that by the 17th century, opium addiction was ubiquitous on a global scale.

In 1805 a French scientist seeking a less addictive form of the drug was able to isolate and extract morphine from opium; codeine came just a few years later. Morphine was used for pain management, as an anesthetic during surgery, and as a treatment for opium addiction until its own addictive properties became evident. In 1874 a pair of English chemists combined morphine with a variety of different acids, eventually synthesizing diacetylmorphine, which the German pharmaceutical company Bayer named *heroin* in 1898.

In the beginning, heroin was proclaimed a miracle drug—four times stronger than morphine and non–habit forming. It was used as a treatment for a variety of common aches and pains and for "women's ailments," including pain during childbirth. Opiates such as codeine were even a commonly found ingredient in cough medicine. But eventually, it became obvious that heroin was as addictive as morphine, and in the United States, Congress banned heroin as abuse skyrocketed.

Methadone, a synthetic opioid compound, dates back to World War II, when German scientists synthesized it as a painkiller for wartime casualties. In 1964 two medical researchers at what is now Rockefeller University, Dr. Vincent Dole and Dr. Marie Nyswander, began testing methadone on heroin addicts who had relapsed after other treatment options failed. During their research, Dole and Nyswander discovered that methadone could block the cravings associated with a heroin habit and, when properly administered, could significantly reduce physical withdrawal. Though Dole and Nyswander recognized the benefit of methadone as a treatment option, they never considered it a silver bullet for curing heroin addiction. In the same way that a person with diabetes relies on regular insulin injections to maintain normal body function, a recovering heroin addict requires regular doses of methadone.

Methadone works by surrounding opioid receptors in the brain and blocking the euphoric effect of heroin and other opiates. It has many of the same pharmacological effects as morphine. Methadone reduces the physical symptoms of withdrawal, including cravings and mood swings. While heroin brings on a sharp rush and crash every three hours, methadone smooths out the dosage cycle through slow onset and a 24-hour half-life. Taking methadone orally just once a day, a heroin-addicted person can live a normal life. Methadone treatment also reduces criminal behavior because it's affordable. A heroin habit costs $200 a day, but a daily dose of methadone costs $13.

Sometimes methadone alone is not able to handle all of an addict's issues. Methadone only blocks the effects of opioids, so non-opioid drugs such as cocaine and alcohol can still be abused. In cases where opioid abuse is combined with other drugs, counseling and/or other psychoactive medications are necessary for an addict to maintain a stable life.

In 1970, New York City faced a major epidemic, with an estimated 200,000 New Yorkers struggling with heroin abuse. It was a true public health emergency, a life-or-death situation. And, as addiction became more and more pervasive, there was a spike in crime, since many addicts turned to robbery, mugging, petty theft, prostitution, and other crimes to support their habit. With public pressure mounting, the mayor and Gordon Chase concluded that methadone maintenance was the best way to help heroin addicts and reduce crime. Chase recruited Dr. Robert Newman, a physician in the NYC Health Department, and together they masterminded a plan to offer methadone to anyone who asked for help.

At the time, there were only a few methadone programs available anywhere. The program screamed for rapid expansion and was a major undertaking demanding an iron will and moral conviction as well as political cunning. The limited number of clinics in the program's early days made for months-long waiting lists, and many addicts died from overdoses, collapsed veins, hepatitis, sepsis and other infections, or criminal behavior while awaiting treatment. Newman, who was young, driven, and super-smart, spearheaded the effort and in just a few years established a citywide program that saved thousands of lives.

Three Seventy-Seven Broadway, headquarters of the city's Methadone Treatment Program, is a nondescript commercial building near a subway station in Lower Manhattan. On a cold January day in 1972, I opened the doors of 377 to report for my first day of work. I was ushered to my little corner of a vast office where I was offered a chair but no desk, but no matter, I'd figure that out. The atmosphere inside 377 was nothing you'd expect from city government. It was a beehive of energy, buzzing with excitement. Like Dr. Newman, the program's fearless leader, the atmosphere was charged and driven, but also friendly and informal. Everyone called each other by their first names, including Dr. Newman, whom we called Bob. Bob had an old, epileptic dog that needed medication several times a day, so he brought him to work. The little dog spent most of the day sleeping under Bob's desk, but whenever Bob raced down the hallway—which he often did—the dog always followed at his heels.

My new boss, Stu Steiner, dropped by to welcome me and along with the welcome told me he'd be leaving his post soon. Then he introduced me to his replacement, David Latham. Steiner also informed me that the Food and Drug Administration and the Justice Department's Bureau of Narcotics and Dangerous Drugs had just shut down two privately owned methadone clinics on the Upper West Side, charging that the owners had been dispensing methadone "indiscriminately." Between them, these clinics treated about 1,500 addicts a day, and in desperation, the city speedily commandeered a retired ferryboat, the *Gold Star Mother*, to serve as a clinic. The *Gold Star Mother* was moored at the foot of the Christopher Street Pier in Greenwich Village and would serve as the makeshift replacement clinic for at least 600 of those displaced addicts. The remaining addicts would be placed in various hospital clinics throughout the city.

Stu handed me a $10 bill. "Grab a cab, go to Pier 45, and keep everything afloat. You're going to oversee the ferryboat operation." I had my first assignment. It wasn't what I expected, but I didn't care. After all, I suddenly had a ferryboat instead of a desk! Mayor Fiorello LaGuardia had launched the *Gold Star Mother* in 1937 and named it for all the mothers who'd lost sons and daughters during World Wars I and II. For over 30 years, the *Gold Star Mother* conveyed people and cars across New York Harbor from Manhattan's Battery to St. George in Staten Island, and now it had been brought out of retirement to serve the city once again.

When I arrived at the pier, it was obvious that the ferryboat was ill-suited to be a methadone clinic. There was a bilge in the middle of the "nursing station" that blew off steam every day like a miniature Old Faithful. The boat lacked private offices for confidential counseling and, worst of all, had very little electrical power. Most of the electricity the *Gold Star Mother* did have was provided by generators. Truth be told, the retired old ferry was barely even suitable as a boat. It listed to one side, and one night it partially sank right there at the pier. Fortunately, our clinic wasn't submerged, and we were able to get the Department of Transportation to refloat the *Gold Star Mother*. The challenges of running a clinic from the ferry were endless, but it was the only space we had, and we were desperate. And I was determined to make it work.

Patients taking methadone are required to have supervised urine tests every week in order to stay in the program, so our first challenge was to provide toilets. I decided the quickest solution would be to place rented portable toilets on deck. I figured out how to make an emergency city purchase so that the toilets arrived in two days. Problem solved . . . or so I thought. Soon we discovered that the hoses of the commercial cleaning trucks used to drain waste from the portable toilets were not long enough to reach the ferry's deck. We needed a quick solution, a plan B, and did the most expeditious thing we could think of: we hired laborers to physically carry the toilets back and forth between dock and ferry.

In the midst of problems, frustrations, and setbacks, I was undaunted. Every new challenge was a joy to me. Every day I learned a bit more about the Health Department and its bureaucracy just by working and observing. I was determined to solve whatever problems, predicaments, or difficulties came my way. When a colleague passed me and asked, "What are you laughing at?" I shrugged. I was deeply immersed, thinking about the job . . . and thinking about my job made me happy. I was obsessed with my work, even at home. My first husband used to notice my mind wandering and say, "Where are you . . . in Methadonia?" Perhaps so, but I just couldn't stay away.

I learned to respect the "green eyeshade people" in the office, some of the most important people in the city because you need their authorization to buy things. Treat them well and they'll expedite your requests; treat them poorly and your requests will wind up on the bottom of the pile. I learned new things every day about drug use, heroin, methadone, and how and why the city's program had become a political issue. Though methadone had already saved the lives of thousands of heroin addicts, the program was highly controversial and faced opposition on several fronts: political, commercial, and even medical. Like many in the African American community, Charles Rangel, the newly elected congressman representing Harlem and the Puerto Rican Barrio in Upper Manhattan, saw methadone as just another addiction and refused to support or have any part of the program.

Another force determined to discredit us was led by privately run drug-free programs and therapeutic communities including Odyssey House, Daytop Village, and Phoenix House, who together mounted a smear campaign against the city's program. They were threatened by the amazing success the city was having in rehabilitating addicts. The other organizations held themselves up as purists and considered their drug-free, abstinence-based treatments the only way addicts could overcome addiction. However, the reality was that their total-abstinence approach failed the vast majority of people in their care. Therapeutic communities only worked when patients lived in the communities' residences, and the long-term results were overwhelmingly poor. Between 80 percent and 90 percent of patients in therapeutic communities relapsed shortly after treatment. Recidivism was the norm, and after months and months of inpatient care, it wasn't long before these addicts were back on the street.

A third opposition force came from within city administration itself. Even as the city's Health Department was expanding the program, reports from the medical examiner's office denounced methadone as a "killer" drug and directly linked it to a growing number of deaths. Dr. Newman was highly skeptical of these reports, since the majority of scientific studies suggested otherwise. For two long years, the media incessantly repeated the story that methadone was a killer, and for two years Newman's demands to see the medical examiner's records on the so-called methadone deaths were denied. Finally, health commissioner Dr. Lowell Bellin allowed Newman access. What he found was astonishing.

Newman discovered that the deputy medical examiner, Dr. Michael Baden, had altered the system of classification so that any death in which a body tested positive for methadone was classified a "methadone-related death." Whether someone was murdered, died in a car accident, or succumbed to cancer, if their remains tested positive for methadone, methadone was cited as the cause of death. In reality, there were virtually no deaths caused by methadone. The media had spent two years extensively reporting fake numbers of "methadone deaths," fomenting a stigma around treatment and causing severe damage to our program's reputation and its ability to help addicts in need.

Once Newman's findings were broadcast, Dr. Milton Helpern, the medical examiner, publicly apologized for the wrongheaded judgment of his deputy, Dr. Baden. Still, Baden was merely admonished, not fired. At the time, Baden was married to Judianne Densen-Gerber, founder of Odyssey House, one of the private programs that had been our aggressive adversaries. Dr. Baden had flagrantly abused his position within the medical examiner's office to help his wife by discrediting methadone as a viable treatment for heroin addiction. Though he'd been exposed, his false reports had so severely damaged the reputation and credibility of the city's program both publicly and politically that it took the program decades to recover.

Sadly, sometimes patients themselves played a part in the public's negative perception of methadone treatment. While an overwhelming majority of our patients arrived at a clinic, took their medication, and went peacefully on their way, there was a small minority, an estimated 25 percent, who abused other drugs, like barbiturates and alcohol, and sometimes socialized right outside. The sight of malingering people nodding out burned an indelibly negative image in the public's mind, and, sadly, methadone became associated with dereliction, not with the accomplishment of so many improved lives.

I spent seven years working to set up methadone clinics, and in those seven years we opened more than 20. I was personally responsible for launching 5 of those clinics and supervised the opening of several others. We eliminated the waiting list and offered treatment to patients on demand. Even with two master's degrees, nothing compared to the education I received in the trenches, so to speak, doing real work. Each new clinic presented a new set of challenges, not the least of which was securing a site and staff. Prejudiced by what they'd heard in the news, most communities objected to having a methadone clinic move into their neighborhood. And finding qualified medical staff willing to work in such an environment was not easy.

The daily reality of clinics was far more ordinary than the sensationalist version reported in the media. A patient's typical experience with a methadone clinic would begin with an initial medical evaluation and exam. Dosing was calculated by how well patients had responded to their current dosage and how frequently they came in for treatment. Patients drank their liquid medication right in front of the nurse and once a week provided a staff-supervised urine sample for drug testing. They met with counselors who reviewed their progress and checked to see if any other drugs showed up in the urine screening. Patients who were clean were given take-home doses. Brand-new patients reported daily in order to gauge their progress as well as their comfort level with initial dosing. Relief from heroin cravings happened immediately. Once methadone dosing reached the normal maintenance level—typically 80 to 100 milligrams (most patients reached dosing stability within a month)—they could return to the clinic three to five days a week.

Talking with addicts, I was struck by the language they used to describe what heroin did for them. They never said they got high; they described the feeling as "getting normal" or "coming back home." Their surprising language spoke volumes to me, and I became convinced that the need for opiates was a physical one stemming from the physiological and chemical states of the body. These addicts weren't seeking a high; they were trying to get back to normal, to stabilize. Their addiction wasn't a moral failing but had developed into a disease that needed to be treated clinically.

Working with the methadone program, I met a wide variety of unique and inspiring people. One of our first patients, Mitzi Mandelbaum, went on to work in the clinics and eventually at our central office. She was over six feet tall and heavyset, with the sweetest, gentlest voice. A lesbian and cross-dresser, she'd had a troubled and difficult life that had led her to heroin addiction. But methadone saved Mitzi and enabled her to completely change the course of her life. She was a sweetheart, a true believer, a valuable witness, and a voluble cheerleader for the program. I'd never encountered anyone like her. Her troubled past hadn't even slightly dampened her spirit, and her enthusiasm was so affecting, you forgot how odd she looked.

Pat Benedetto ran one of our clinics in Queens. He'd once owned a famous bar, Googie's, in Greenwich Village, but had gotten involved with illicit drugs and become an addict. When he entered the methadone program, his life turned around, and Pat went from down-and-out junkie to law-school graduate. When he was preparing to join the New York State Bar Association, he decided to be totally honest and reveal his ongoing methadone treatment. After serious discussion, the Bar Association approved him, advancing the acceptance of methadone as a legitimate medical treatment one step further.

Then there was Maurice. Maurice Battle was a young African American man who was savvy, handsome, gay, and always meticulously dressed. While some of my colleagues dressed down when visiting clinics, especially clinics in lower-income, crime-prone neighborhoods, Maurice dressed up. I took my lead from him. Once, when we went to visit a clinic on 118th Street in Harlem, I felt every eye track us as we walked down the block. Dressed in a sharp dark blue suit and carrying a long, precisely wrapped umbrella, Maurice walked with a strut. A little boy gawked at him as he approached, and Maurice stopped short, towering over the boy like some fantastic, regal statue. Maurice tilted his head forward slightly and, glaring down at the child without breaking the elegant line of his pose, said commandingly, "Why are you not in school?" Without a peep, the child turned and ran, and I saw several people on the street nod toward Maurice in agreement and with obvious respect.

In 1973 I was assigned to open a contracted clinic that was to be run by New York Hospital on Manhattan's Upper East Side. Working with the hospital staff, we found a suitable storefront nearby, renovated it to serve as a clinic, and began accepting patients. After the first director left the job, I got a call from an administrator at New York Hospital wanting us to approve a young man to be hired as the new director. Under the city's contract with the hospital, our staff had to review and approve the new hire. When I heard their candidate's name, I recognized him as a man we had recently fired for incompetence from another of our clinics. I explained this to the hospital administrators, and we rejected the candidate.

A few days later, I received a call from an African American senior hospital physician inviting me to dinner. Unsuspecting, I accepted his invitation. He picked me up in a splendid Rolls-Royce, and we drove to a high-end restaurant on the Upper East Side. As we dined, the doctor tried to convince me to change my mind about the hiring decision. I told him no, and once again explained my reasons. He then changed the subject and asked me if I enjoyed my job, and I went on and on about how much I loved my work. Yet the evening grew more and more uncomfortable as my dinner companion appeared to become more and more frustrated. Finally, the meal was over and he drove me home.

The next morning, I told Maurice about my awkward evening. He knew the doctor was one of the most prominent Black physicians from Harlem Hospital and explained that his question about whether I enjoyed my job had actually been a veiled threat. It never dawned on me that "Do you enjoy your job?" actually meant "Hire my guy, or else you might lose it." Fortunately, nothing ever came of it, but I learned another lesson about the world.

In 1975, as New York plummeted into one of the worst fiscal crises in the city's history, the French and Polyclinic Hospital on West 51st Street went bankrupt and was forced to close its doors. We had a methadone clinic there that was treating about 400 addicts. At the 11th hour, the hospital had received a shipment of thousands of methadone tablets we couldn't afford to lose. Certainly, we could place patients in other treatment programs, but we couldn't afford to lose that much of a valuable, highly restricted and regulated drug. Maurice and I acted on instinct—we raced up to the hospital on the afternoon it was scheduled to close and swept through the clinic bagging dozens and dozens of bottles of methadone pills in black plastic garbage bags. As the doors shut behind us for the last time, and with bags slung over our shoulders like Santa, we were overcome with laughter at how ridiculous we must appear. We smuggled our loot to Seventh Avenue, hailed a taxi, and headed back to the office. Only when we arrived did we realize that we'd broken the law! Nevertheless, we were pleased with ourselves for liberating all those lifesaving doses of methadone. Were we young and stupid? Yes. But we were also very proud of our salvage effort.

Another time, I was assigned to negotiate a contract for a new methadone clinic at Bellevue Hospital. I admit this threw me for a loop, since after all, Bellevue is as iconic and legendary an institution as can be. Founded in 1736, it was the first public hospital in the United States, and its very name is synonymous with all of healthcare history, including psychiatry, mayhem, and crime. Bellevue was the site of the first New York City medical examiner's office, as well as the first educational site for training thousands of physicians and nurses. I made an appointment and set off toward 30th Street and First Avenue. I had finally found the nearly hidden long alleyway that led to the administrative offices when a naked man came running wildly at me, two orderlies close behind. I jumped to the side and squeezed myself against the wall as all three whizzed by. The orderlies caught up with the man and walked him back, and I recovered enough to get to my appointment. *Hmm*, I thought, *so this is Bellevue. It certainly doesn't disappoint. . . .*

A few years later, when Peter and I were about to marry, I decided to give up my two-bedroom apartment on West 102nd Street. Maurice and his partner happened to be looking for a new apartment at that time, so I recommended them to the landlord. When Maurice came in to fill out an application, the landlord immediately refused him. The reason was obvious, so I went to speak to the landlord to see if I could reverse the decision. I sang Maurice's praises, and eventually he relented and Maurice and his partner moved in. But in 1976 it was clear that racial bias was still alive and well in what was, even then, a marginal neighborhood. The truth hurts.

At another point, the clinics I was supervising were having a lot of trouble making corrections in the computerized medication system. Try as they might, the nurses' dosage updates didn't register. I discussed the issue several times with the computer managers in our central office, and they insisted that the clinic nurses were entering the information incorrectly and were just plain dumb. I went to a clinic and watched the nurses enter their corrections myself. I waited a week for updates to appear, but there was still no change. I returned to the clinic and noticed that the printed heading on the computer medication schedule that instructed them to set the change for a certain date was two weeks later than the date of the current schedule. Then I went back to the central office and examined that system. We realized that the written instructions on the nurses' medication sheets were wrong: the computer schedules' written instructions were off by a week. The computer managers were finally chagrined. They corrected the instructions, and from then on, updates and changes registered correctly. It was another valuable lesson: *Question everything, assume nothing*—a lesson I've never forgotten.

One afternoon in 1975, I was reading *Serpico*, the account of corruption in the New York City Police Department that was currently topping the best-seller list. Deep into the book, a name jumped off the page: Carmelo (Gil) Zumatto. The book described Gil as an extraordinarily smart and capable bagman for the corrupt detectives of the South Bronx. I was stunned. I'd been working with Gil for two years, and he was a terrific colleague, extremely capable, with enormous potential. When we met, he was working for Ramon Velez, a notoriously powerful, politically connected operator in the South Bronx. Velez headed the Hunts Point Multi-Service Center, which focused primarily on healthcare but offered other programs too. Gil had been assigned to assist me in opening a methadone clinic at Hunts Point, and certainly the man described in *Serpico* did not match the man I knew. I was determined to talk with him about it and a few weeks later brought it up over lunch.

Gil acknowledged that the events described in *Serpico* had happened during a very bad period in his life. By the time Frank Serpico blew the whistle, Gil was a 14-year veteran of the NYPD. His precinct was steeped in corruption, and Gil had just gone along with it. In the book, even Frank Serpico noted that if Gil had put his energies into something legitimate, he'd have been enormously successful. But with the fallout from *Serpico*, Gil was given a stark choice: he could resign and give up his pension or face criminal charges. He chose the former.

The book destroyed him. His family abandoned him, he lost his reputation, and no one would hire him. Gil was a broken man who finally got a job as a taxi dispatcher in the Bronx. Ramon Velez hired him to work for his organization and then assigned him to work with me. I pressed Gil to get away from Hunts Point and encouraged him to earn his bachelor's and master's degrees, which he did. When he dedicated his master's thesis to me many years later, I was more than proud. Gil went on to found and run the nonprofit agency Bronx Addiction Services Integrated Concepts System (BASICS), and we remained good friends until he passed away in his mid-70s.

My experience working in the methadone program was an immersive education in government, public health, addiction, effective management, and community relations. It was the best training I could possibly have had. Dr. Newman was a brilliant administrator and a fierce champion of methadone maintenance who was determined that the program help as many people as it possibly could. He was one of the first administrators to utilize city contracts to expedite and extend the reach of government programs, and was also one of the first to design a computer system that scrupulously maintained a potentially lifesaving waiting list, as well as one that monitored the methadone usage of each patient: every dose, every day, in every clinic. All the while, Dr. Newman challenged the heavy regulations imposed on methadone by the FDA and DEA.

After six years working with the Methadone Maintenance Treatment Program for the city, he was offered a senior position at Beth Israel Hospital, where he became an international expert on addiction and methadone treatment. Dr. Newman never looked back. By the time he retired almost 30 years later, he was the head of Continuum Health Care, a vast private healthcare and hospital consortium that included five major New York City hospitals.

Driven in part by the desperate financial situation choking the city, Mayor Lindsay's successor, Abe Beame, began dismantling all the "super-agencies" built during the Lindsay administration. John Lindsay had a modern vision for city government that required reorganizing multiple agencies into a few powerhouses. He established the Addiction Services Agency to oversee all drug treatment options other than methadone. It would administer all city-contracted, community-based, drug-free services. When Beame dissolved Addiction Services, most of its functions were absorbed into the "old" Health Department. That's when I got my deputy commissioner title. After Dr. Newman left, Dr. Bernard Bihari ran the methadone program and also became responsible for the newly absorbed Addiction Services. Bihari and I worked together to reduce staff overhead.

I made some lifelong friends at the methadone program, and chief among them was Paul Roth. Paul and I had started at the same time and held parallel jobs opening and monitoring clinics. At one point Paul left for a hospital administrative job, but when we inherited Addiction Services, I reached out to him to work with me, and Paul returned to city government. We worked hard to reform the whole system, Paul reforming finance while I streamlined programs. Addiction Services had hundreds of contracts with community agencies for prevention, drug education, and drug-free treatment. There were the dominant drug-free agencies, like Phoenix House, Odyssey House, Project Return, and Samaritan House, as well as numerous other small community agencies, all of which operated autonomously and unsupervised.

We became quite unpopular as we began to rein them in and put financial and programmatic requirements in place. We brought contracts up to date and established contract standards that had to be adhered to. We eliminated unnecessary paperwork and reduced administrative costs. Unfortunately, we also had to lay off city employees. I revoked dozens of city cars assigned to agency staff; they'd been a major perk, and one deputy commissioner, a former professional football player, raised himself to his full height and rattled his desk at me when I took his car keys away. There was one assistant commissioner who continually undermined our efforts, and even though we knew he was "protected" by Queens borough president Donald Manes, we fired him. We waited for City Hall to order us to reinstate him, but the order never came.

Despite our best efforts, in 1977 the city's fiscal crisis was unrelenting, and in order to save more money and further reduce payroll, the city announced it was transferring the entire Addiction Services Agency to the state. My job and dozens of others would be eliminated.

Postscript: Methadonia

IN 2016 A NEW HEROIN AND OPIOID EPIDEMIC began raging through the United States in a crisis far more insidious and deadly than New York City's heroin epidemic decades before. Because of the availability and frequent illegal peddling of prescription opiates, addiction has captured the suburbs and small towns of America, tightening its sinister grip even before its victims know what's happening to them. Doctors overprescribe, patients overuse and become addicted, and the sons and daughters of unsuspecting and helpless American families are overdosing and dying in large numbers. When prescriptions run out or money dries up, inexpensive heroin can fill the void. Cheap heroin is plentiful on the street—cheaper, even, than opiate pills. Equally devastating is a new drug called fentanyl, which is widely available and often cut with street heroin.

Mercifully, this new epidemic has been recognized by state and federal governments, and as of this writing, nationwide addiction treatment is expanding. Once again, methadone is widely considered one of the most effective solutions for overcoming heroin and opioid addiction and remains the standard for success.

CHAPTER 2

HUMAN RESOURCES ADMINISTRATION

The Belly of the Beast

I WAS INTRODUCED TO BOB TROBE one evening at a party. Trobe was the new deputy commissioner at the Human Resources Administration, and, hearing that I was looking for a job, he asked me to come in and interview for a high-level position he was trying to fill. The interview evolved into one big argument over how he should reorganize his division of HRA, but Bob enjoyed our discussion so much he offered me the job as his assistant deputy. For the next seven years, I'd need every ounce of my acquired knowledge, experience, and creative energy.

The Human Resources Administration is the mother of all bureaucracies. The brainchild of Mayor John Lindsay's administration, the formation of HRA was part and parcel of an initiative to consolidate numerous city agencies into a few mega power centers, or super-agencies. HRA was the biggest of all, having absorbed Welfare, Addiction Services, Youth Development, and Manpower Development, which was designed to train people for work. Welfare alone included Income Maintenance, Medicaid, Adult Services, and Children's Services, as well the numerous subdivisions of those services. Under one roof, HRA would manage New York City's vast social services empire. The Lindsay planners believed the super-agencies would streamline services, render day-to-day operations more efficient, and, of course, bring down expenses. Inevitably, the newly

configured agencies were ripe for plum patronage jobs the administration would deliver to favored supporters, and at HRA there were
lots of jobs. HRA employed 25,000 people and had a budget of $3.9
billion, which was then about 30 percent of the entire New York
City budget.

The largest agency folded into HRA was the Department of Welfare, which provided 1.3 million New Yorkers with weekly welfare
checks. It supervised a constellation of welfare centers, plus the food
stamp and Medicaid programs. HRA also absorbed Welfare's adop-
tion and foster-care programs, the investigation of child abuse, and
tracking down deadbeat dads. And HRA would oversee a rapidly
growing program that provided home care for tens of thousands of
elderly New Yorkers, and manage the city's 300 senior citizen centers, as well as a host of other services for vulnerable senior citizens.

HRA was a bureaucratic monster, a world unto itself. It was responsible for the most complex, intractable, and often distasteful
aspects of big-city life. Leading the agency during its early years
was Mitchell Ginsberg, who'd earned the nickname "Give It Away
Ginsberg" because he was at the helm when "welfare on demand"
was instituted. "Welfare on demand" meant that bureaucratic hurdles to receiving benefits were eliminated—causing welfare rolls to
explode. HRA was indeed crucial to the survival of thousands of
New Yorkers, but it was also the notorious target of criticism and
political debate—about Medicaid, about food stamps and welfare
"cheats," about vagrants (not yet known as "the homeless"), and
even about deadbeat dads. Many functions were given shiny new
names. To New York liberals, the term *welfare* was considered de-
meaning, so it became Income Maintenance. And the Bureau of
Child Welfare was renamed Special Services for Children until it
was finally called the Administration for Children's Services, or
ACS. You might not solve the problem, but you can always give it a
new name, a benign camouflage to obscure poor past performance
or bad press.

I was hired as assistant deputy administrator, and my last job title
at HRA was deputy administrator. Our division, Family and Adult
Services (FAS), was run by Robert Trobe. FAS supervised home

care, services for the homeless, senior citizen centers, family planning clinics, protective services for adults, adult homes, and in fact, all programs for adult New Yorkers except income maintenance. Trobe was an amazing manager and leader. Creative and thoughtful, he was a true change agent and an inspiration to his staff. The first time I walked into his office, Bob stood up, shook my hand, and said, "Welcome to the belly of the beast," and I quickly learned exactly what he meant.

When I arrived, Trobe had been at FAS for about six months. His father, Jake, was the executive director of the Jewish Child Care Association, a widely respected nonprofit agency. His mother, Adele, also worked in social services, including a stint with Planned Parenthood. Trobe loved challenge, and he knew something about the social services field. He told us he'd been a schoolteacher but had been totally defeated by kids running wild in his class. And you could see why—he was a dreamer and an intellectual and a passionate opera fan. His shirt was always flying out of his trousers, his glasses were always smudged, and in the seven years he worked at HRA, he was never even sure which way to turn to go to his office when he got off the elevator. He was also a political junkie who knew the status of every election in every state.

Bob Trobe was constantly thinking and talking, inspiring and engaging a staff who adored him. In 1978 he told us our department faced two major challenges: first, the city's out-of-control home-care program, which provided 10,000 elderly and disabled New Yorkers care in their own homes through aides or attendants. Home care was a wildly popular program that had grown rapidly but was horribly disorganized. It was so badly managed that aides were paid unconscionably late and sometimes had to wait six months for a check. Bob told us that home care needed to be overhauled from top to bottom, and that it was up to us to do it.

The other major challenge was homelessness, which no one yet understood. Chronic homelessness was just beginning to develop on the streets of New York, and in 1978, no one could have foretold the tragic story of homelessness that would engulf and overwhelm New York City in the 1980s and beyond.

Providing Shelter

THE HOMELESS HAVE ALWAYS BEEN AMONG US. Every town, every city has a population of alcoholics, the mentally ill, skid-row bums, and vagrants; people in transition, people living on the "other side of the tracks." But until the '70s in New York City, the homeless were known simply as bums and were usually alcoholic white men living a marginal existence in the Bowery in Lower Manhattan. And there were a mere handful of "bag ladies" with their trademark shopping carts. At that time, too, tens of thousands of New Yorkers were living in state mental hospitals, and enormous mental institutions were located all over the state.

However, in the late 1960s, when psychopharmacological medications began to be used to stabilize the mentally ill, instead of warehousing people in institutions, thousands were discharged into the world, often with absolutely nowhere to go. It was a desperate time, and the understanding and resources necessary to accomplish sudden transitions from institution to community were painfully slow to emerge. Many older mentally ill people were sent to unprepared nursing homes; others were discharged to single-room-occupancy hotels (SROs), mostly on the Upper West Side of Manhattan. As the city began to recover from the fiscal crisis in the mid-'70s, the real estate market was the first to revive, and one by one, each of those single-occupancy hotels was gutted and turned into upscale housing. At HRA, Bob Jorgen, who headed Crisis Intervention Services (CIS), which provided help to vulnerable SRO residents, repeatedly sounded the alarm, warning that a crisis was brewing, but nobody listened. As each hotel shut down, residents were moved into vacancies in other buildings until, by 1980, there was no more room at the inn. If SROs had been hellholes, they were at least hellholes hidden from public view. When those buildings began to be renovated for luxury housing, the displaced people visibly spilled into the streets, and the "homeless crisis" began.

Meanwhile, other housing options started to disappear. Rooming houses and cheap hotels all over the city vanished.

From the *New York Times*, August 6, 1976: "The Bowery scene has spread. In late hours vagrants can now be found in twos and threes in the triangles on Broadway from Herald Square to 72nd Street, along the southern edge of Central Park, in the side streets of Times Square, around the fountained plazas of the Avenue of the Americas, along Lexington Avenue above 42nd Street, in the small parks of the Lower East Side and in Trinity Place." Hundreds were living in the streets and in subway cars and stations. There were encampments in the subway and in railroad tunnels. As the city's financial health increased, so did the homeless population. Prosperity only exacerbated homelessness, as affordable housing disappeared and the moniker *homeless* replaced *Bowery bum, wacko,* or *street person.*

The City's involvement in housing those without a place to live dated back to the Great Depression, when city, state, and federal governments had to deal with massive unemployment. But when World War II began, the Depression lifted and the need for shelter markedly diminished. When I joined FAS in 1978, HRA's homeless programs were centered in three locations. One was a men's shelter housed in a large, four-story building on East Third Street between Second and Third Avenues on the Lower East Side. But this was not a true shelter, since capacity was limited and only a handful of men could stay overnight. Still, hundreds came in every day for three hot meals and rudimentary healthcare. The men gathered in what became known as the Big Room on the first floor, and every afternoon they lined up for a voucher, or chit, which bought them a night's sleep in one of the nearby flophouses in the Bowery. The men's shelter supported hundreds of homeless men every day, yet it was also a contradiction—both lifesaving and perilous at the same time.

The shelter was cavernous, so the noise was overwhelming, echoing everywhere. And the smell was almost unbearable. A visit to the shelter conjured thoughts of Dante's Inferno, and the realities the shelter staff dealt with day in and day out were, more often than not, disturbing and dangerous. The staff did the best they could in almost intolerable circumstances. I remember one unsung hero, shelter director Calvin Reid. Calvin attended a community meeting to hear neighbors' complaints that East Third Street smelled like a urinal. In utter exasperation, he told the crowd, "I resent the notion that East Third Street smells like a urinal. Actually, the whole neighborhood smells like urine, not only East Third Street." Reid was booed out of the room.

The other shelter for men was far away from the city, 60 miles north in Orange County. Camp LaGuardia was on 300 acres, and about 800 homeless men were housed there, most of them older, now-sober alcoholics who could no longer withstand the rigors of street life. During the area's busy summer vacation season, some of them were employed as dishwashers and laborers. Camp LaGuardia served as a kind of retirement home almost, a serene place to spend one's waning years. Built in 1918, the camp was originally Greycourt, a women's prison and "farm colony." In 1934, during the Great Depression, the city converted it into a shelter for unemployed men, and in 1935 it was renamed Camp LaGuardia, after Fiorello LaGuardia, New York City's mayor. During the Depression, a farm on the property grew produce, supplying many schools and hospitals in the city.

Camp LaGuardia had two remarkable features that caught my attention. One was the Tap Room, a small bar that served beer to those men the staff thought could handle it. When he was going through the homeless section of the annual city budget in the 1980s, Owen Fitzgerald, a New York *Daily News* reporter, came across an expenditure item for a Tap Room—cases of beer for Camp LaGuardia. He thought, *This can't be right*, so he called our press office. But our press people had never heard of a Tap Room in a homeless shelter either, so they did some research and to their amazement discovered that the Camp LaGuardia Tap Room was a fact. They called Fitzgerald back to let him know and told him that the Tap Room was considered a small perk for men nearing the end of their days. The reporter kindly let it slide and never wrote a word about it.

A second remarkable feature was the ice house. Anyone who died during the winter was kept in the ice house because the ground was frozen and they couldn't be buried . . . just a fact of life. With the spring thaw, the "ice room" men were finally buried on the grounds.

But when the homeless population exploded in the 1980s, the profile of the men at Camp LaGuardia began to change. We built two new dormitories in 1982, expanding capacity to 1,000 beds. Older, more subdued residents were joined by younger, more difficult men, and the locals began to be distressed about Camp LaGuardia. Ironically, many of the locals were New York City firefighters and cops who'd moved upstate just to avoid this indigent population. The town of Chester began to resent the camp.

A third city shelter was the women's shelter in a building on Lafayette Street in Lower Manhattan. It had only 46 beds but served three hot meals a day and provided social services to the relatively few fortunate women who were able to call it home. The shelter was run by Robert White, a social worker who in later years would manage the entire homeless program for the city. Bob was the saintliest person I've ever known. Competent, compassionate, and religious, he was one of those unique civil servants born in the South, who, after serving in the military, moved to New York in the late 1950s. When Bob informed us that more than 600 "bag ladies" were turned away from shelters every year because there was simply no room for them, it set off alarms. When we told HRA administrator Dr. Blanche Bernstein (who held rather conservative views on welfare) about the hundreds of street women turned away, she instructed us to "go find another place for them as soon as you possibly can," and we quickly converted a vacant school building in Bushwick, Brooklyn, into a shelter for about 150 women. The opening of such a significant facility in just a matter of weeks was unheard of, but our leadership and staff were totally inspired, and the new shelter was up and running in almost no time.

In 1979 our shelter population in the four locations was approximately 1,500 single men and women. We would never have believed that by 2019, the homeless single adult population would grow to 17,000. As of 2020, the New York City shelter system housed almost 60,000 men, women, and children every night ... and the numbers keep going up.

One day in 1979, a young man named Robert Hayes came to see us. He was an attorney for Sullivan & Cromwell, one of New York's most prestigious law firms. Hayes had become friendly with a man named Robert Callahan who lived on the streets. Callahan was ill, and in a few weeks he died. Hayes was so outraged by Callahan's helplessness and suffering that he was determined to do something to prevent this from happening to anyone again. What Robert Hayes did would change the face of homelessness in New York City forever.

We began discussions with Hayes about sheltering the homeless but could not come to an understanding. Hayes wanted us to guarantee shelter to all homeless men, arguing that the New York State Constitution commanded it. The city argued that there was, in fact, no city or state requirement and that, while the constitution did prescribe support of indigent individuals, it did not necessarily require the city to provide shelter. On December 5, 1979, Robert Hayes filed a class action suit in New York State Supreme Court, *Callahan v. Carey* (Hugh Carey was governor of New York), against the city and state on behalf of all street-dwelling men. *Callahan v. Carey* claimed that the New York State Constitution prescribed a right to shelter and required the city to shelter homeless men who applied. Hayes cited Article 17 as an implied right to shelter: "The aid, care and support of the needy are public concerns and shall be provided by the State and by such of its subdivisions, and in such a manner and by such means, as the legislature may from time to time determine."

At this point the city, HRA, and FAS—and to some extent the state also—claimed "no room at the inn." The case dragged on before Judge Andrew Tyler. Also in opposition to Bob Hayes and his organization, the Coalition for the Homeless, were numerous politicians afraid that a homeless shelter would open in their neighborhood. When an injunction by Judge Tyler mandated us to immediately house 750 more men, we did so by commandeering state armories and vacant space on Wards Island.

The deck was badly stacked against us, and eventually we reached the obvious consensus that a protracted lawsuit against homeless men by the City of New York was not good public policy and agreed to a consent decree. We haggled with the coalition about the precise wording, but on August 26, 1981, Mayor Koch signed a consent decree. (Later there'd be other agreements to house women, and then families.) In the end, of course, the city got very little credit from either the press or the coalition for voluntarily signing a document agreeing to provide shelter for any homeless man who requested it.

After the consent decree was signed, the floodgates opened, and sheltering the homeless consumed every second of our time. We couldn't open shelters fast enough, and we were flat-out running 24/7 in emergency mode. Opening shelters was logistics, logistics, logistics: procuring beds, pillows, sheets, and blankets for hundreds and hundreds of people and opening shelter after shelter. But we felt good about our work because the need truly was urgent and we were making a difference in homeless people's lives.

Given the community opposition to shelters, it's a miracle we were able to live up to the terms of the decree at all. The City of New York deserves enormous credit for tackling this mandate to house all the homeless, and succeeding. Though it was a huge struggle, NYC housed every person who asked for help. Even today, when thousands of single adults refuse care and remain on the streets, every one of them is known by name to the social workers and police who frequently try to coax them in out of the cold.

By contrast, the homeless situations in Los Angeles, San Francisco, and Seattle are desperately out of control. Only New York has so diligently and successfully managed this challenge. No other city in the United States invests as much in its homeless population. At FAS, we became a battle-hardened team that achieved results despite the often-brutal public and personal criticism that rained down. But we were tireless and undefeated, and we loved and respected one another like soldiers in the trenches.

The state gave us the use of the empty Keener Building on the grounds of the Manhattan State Psychiatric Center on Wards Island as our first additional shelter. The Wards Island facility could house 400 men. Some of them had once been patients at Manhattan State and had come full circle to return as shelter residents. The Bushwick women's shelter was the first truly significant expansion of the shelter system for women in over 25 years. However, when the surrounding community found out about it, they protested . . . loudly. When Bob O'Brien, a scrappy reporter for *Channel 5 News*, called, I was assigned to talk to him. In the course of our conver-

sation, he discovered that I had not personally been to the site, a
fact he gleefully announced on air, and I was slammed for being a
"disconnected," out-of-touch bureaucrat. I was publicly embarrassed
but learned immediately about the bite and power of the press, and
after that, I was always prepared. I credit O'Brien for teaching me a
hard but invaluable lesson.

Every week we provided thousands of bedsheets for our shelters,
and it wasn't long before the supply deputy commissioner for HRA,
Bob Riley, and our operations chief, Wilbur Hicks, were at each
other's throats over the quantity and expense of the sheets. Wilbur needed more, but Riley thought he'd ordered enough. I called a
Kafkaesque meeting with them one Friday afternoon to analyze the
"life cycle of a sheet in the New York City shelter system." The men
were so angry at each other an altercation seemed inevitable. But
after bulging neck veins and fighting words, we finally came to an
agreement. A few weeks later, we discovered the root of the problem:
months earlier, each of the commercial laundries who washed our
sheets had decided they didn't want to mingle shelter sheets with
those of their hotel customers any longer. We then arranged for the
sheets to be laundered on Rikers Island, where prisoners worked in a
huge laundry facility for the jails. But when the clean sheets destined
for our shelters were bundled up, prison guards would bayonet the
bales to be sure that no prisoners were smuggling themselves out of
Rikers. In the process, our sheets were practically destroyed.

Over three years, from 1980 to 1983, we created 5,000 beds in
shelters for homeless men and women. From experience, we learned
that if we announced beforehand that we were opening a shelter in a
neighborhood, we'd be opposed by elected officials and the community and hard-pressed to succeed. But we had to meet the mandate
of the consent decree, so we decided not to announce our intentions,
and to move into shelter buildings in the dead of night. When the
neighborhood woke up in the morning to find a men's shelter in their
midst, they were *not* happy.

But homeless men streamed in by the hundreds, by the thousands, and we commandeered New York State armories one after
the other. We used old school buildings. We built new buildings, like

the one on Wards Island. We considered a federal surplus building, but when a local congressman heard about it, he blocked our way. It was a super-tough 24/7 slog, with the consent decree dogging us all the way. We were excoriated by outraged communities as well as our own City Budget Office, since we kept exceeding our budget. We were pulled into court, and after a second lawsuit, *McCain v. Koch*, mandatory sheltering of women was included in the court order.

Single adults sheltered by the city more than doubled from 2,155 in 1980 to 5,065 in 1983. Meeting the challenge of opening and sustaining such a vast shelter system, you need extraordinary people, and one of most extraordinary was Charles H. Gay. Without his leadership and the round-the-clock work of his formidable staff, known as Charlie's Army, we could never have met the demand for shelter that exploded in New York City in the early 1980s, and we wouldn't have stood a chance of complying with the consent decree.

Charles Gay was wise, dedicated, and terrific at running the operations of all the city's homeless shelters. He was one in a million, but you would never know it to look at him. He was a short, overweight, African American family man in crumpled brown suits who chain-smoked, drank too much coffee, and worked way too many hours. Charlie hardly spoke, but when he let out a suppressed laugh, shrugged his shoulders, or raised an eyebrow in response to a suggested solution that would probably not work, you got the message right away.

Charlie was born in North Carolina in 1931 and grew up there before joining the army. After the army, where he reached the rank of lieutenant, Charlie said farewell to North Carolina forever and moved to New York City. He got married, raised a family, and bought a house in Brooklyn, and eventually Charlie bought a new Cadillac every couple of years. He started out as a caseworker working his way up the civil service ladder in the old Department of Welfare. He shrewdly joined the Madison Democratic Club, one of the strongest old-style political clubs in town.

When impoverished ghettos were proliferating all over the United States and President Johnson declared his "War on Poverty," tons of money began rolling in from the federal government. Control of the money and the hiring of vast numbers of people went to the new War on Poverty organizations, and the local, old-fashioned political clubs became obsolete. Then, instead of joining a club to network and further their careers, the best and the brightest made big bucks working for the War on Poverty. Still, Charlie stayed put in the old clubhouse world. While the new players ignored him, his work on the homeless at HRA in the early 1980s would vault Charlie to the absolute forefront of public policy.

Charlie was just one of many Black men from the South who'd enlisted in the armed forces, gone to college on the GI Bill, then moved to New York to make their mark. By the late '70s, Charlie was at FAS directing the still fairly small homeless shelter system. And since city government provided plenty of opportunity, many of the top lieutenants in Charlie's Army—including Wilbur Hicks, Bob White, Ed Austin, Larry Millender, Crosby Inman, Calvin Reid, and Hy Burton—had taken that exact same route. Bob Trobe and I knew and worked with them all.

The genius of Trobe was his team approach. No matter what the task, Bob made sure the solution was in competent hands. Being part of one of Bob's teams was fantastic, and everybody thrived amidst the support, enthusiasm, and brainpower of the team. There was virtually no backbiting, so we moved expertly from task to task. Our goals were clear. It was hard work, but it was exhilarating.

The expansion of the shelter system, a labor-intensive, 24-hour-a-day enterprise, gave Charlie Gay a chance to hire large numbers of underemployed, who under his guidance found useful paid work. Charlie loved providing jobs and opportunities and was an old-fashioned boss, tough but fair. He expected the men and women who worked for him to work as hard as he did. If you didn't, you wouldn't last long in Charlie's Army. He suffered no fools, but his word was gold and you could depend on it.

Once Mayor Koch asked Charlie how long he would need to set up an outreach team. Charlie didn't hesitate: *three days*. Koch looked at him incredulously. *I could do it in two if necessary*. The mayor looked shocked. He had never heard a civil servant respond so quickly and emphatically, but that was Charlie. Through numerous

lieutenants, Charlie kept his finger on the pulse of the entire city system. He knew what was happening in every shelter, knew each one's
strengths and weaknesses. Involved in every detail of opening a new
shelter, he and his staff helped evaluate possible sites we'd located, to
which the mayor's office then had to give the green light.

When we were offered a federal bachelor officers' quarters in Fort
Totten, Queens, we stealthily dropped Wilbur Hicks, a former para-
trooper, in by helicopter so that the neighbors wouldn't see the HRA
vans. But the feds rescinded their offer after a local congressman
heard about the plan from the military. When we finally did have
a site, we moved quickly making renovations, working with the fire
department to ensure that the building was safe, making certain that
the HVAC was functioning and that all the plumbing was in working order. We requisitioned beds, mattresses, pillows, and sheets. We
assembled 24-hour staffing and security and established a sanitation
schedule. If there was a kitchen program, food was ordered, along
with plates, cups, glasses, and eating utensils. Cooks and kitchen
staff had to be hired, every Health Department standard had to be
met, and all this before a single homeless person could walk through
the door. Then arrangements were made to transport men who con-
vened at the East Third Street shelter to the new site.

Beginning in 1979 with the 150-bed Bushwick women's shelter,
week after week, month after month, Charlie and his army opened
new facilities. Later in 1979, the state awarded us a part of the
shuttered Manhattan State Psychiatric Center on Wards Island.
Whereas the Keener Building on Wards Island first housed 400
homeless men, occupancy doubled in early 1982 when we constructed a new building on the same grounds. The new building
was named Schwarz after Don Schwarz, the late CEO of Volun-
teers of America. VOA was the first nonprofit in the city to offer us
their services. Service was their mission too, and they were pleased
to contribute. We built the Schwarz building in six months by
funneling capital funds through an emergency VOA shelter contract and constructing it with private builders. The building was
designed and supervised by city architects but would have taken
years to actually put up if the city had had to construct it in com-

pliance with the Wicks Law and other typically labyrinthine laws and regulations.

Month after month, year after year, we kept opening shelters. The numbers of homeless people only increased. Three hundred fifty homeless men were sheltered in the East New York shelter, an unused school in East New York, Brooklyn. When the Board of Elections informed us that they used that building for voting, we just cleared out the first floor for voting stations.

On the night of February 4, 1982, a television reporter called HRA to report that a homeless woman in her 80s, believed to be suffering from gangrene, was in dire need of medical assistance at Grand Central Station. HRA commissioner Jack Krauskopf was notified and alerted our staff. He also called Mayor Koch at home in Gracie Mansion, and both of them headed for Grand Central, arriving at about 11:45 p.m. They tried to persuade the lady—later identified as Mary O'Hanlon—to go to a hospital, but she refused. But before leaving, Commissioner Krauskopf and Mayor Koch spoke with Bob Trobe. Trobe contacted Charlie Gay at his home to see if anything else could be done. Gay's first call was to Robert Reich, HRA director of psychiatric services, who immediately drove to the station from his home in Great Neck, Long Island. When he arrived and examined Ms. O'Hanlon, he found her to be malnourished and disoriented, and he issued an order for her temporary commitment to Bellevue.

Meanwhile, just before 2 a.m., while awaiting word about the fate of Mary O'Hanlon, Charlie began to have difficulty breathing. His wife, Mary, called 911, and Charlie was rushed to Kings County Hospital in Brooklyn, where he died at 3:35 am ... at just about the same time Mary O'Hanlon was admitted to Bellevue. The following morning, Mayor Koch issued this statement:

Charlie Gay's actions early this morning on behalf of a homeless woman who was in danger and in need of care [were] typical of his work on behalf of the homeless people in our city. As a committed public servant Charlie cared deeply about the well-being of these men and women and worked tirelessly to make their lives a little better.

When we arrived at work, we learned of Charles Gay's death. So many tears were shed, it was one the blackest of days for the entire agency and, very personally, for me. In honor of Charlie, we named the Wards Island complex the Charles H. Gay Shelter for Homeless Men. To this day, the building named for Charlie still shelters hundreds.

During the Koch administration, deputy mayor Nat Leventhal had the thankless job of overseeing all the operations of city government 24 hours a day, every day of the year. Since the homeless issue was now one of the most important policy issues facing the Koch administration, we dealt closely with Leventhal and his staff, often on a daily basis. Leventhal came up with an idea for us: instead of opening one shelter at a time, try opening three in one night—one in Brooklyn, one in the Bronx, and one in Manhattan. We had already identified several sites in each of the boroughs: an unused school in Brooklyn, an armory in the Bronx, and, most remarkably, the 69th Regiment Armory on Park Avenue, in Manhattan's wealthy Upper East Side. Imagine a shelter for the homeless on Park Avenue, right in the heart of the city's richest neighborhood. A shelter on Park Avenue would send the message that we were not exclusively targeting poor or working-class neighborhoods for shelter sites. But if we felt that this made us appear more egalitarian or stood us on some higher moral ground, it made no difference at all when communities erupted in anger over a shelter in their neighborhood.

Leventhal had to deal with a slew of other issues, authorizing not just shelters but prisons, waste disposal sites, sanitation garages— things no neighborhood wanted. His staff had a button made up for him: DEPUTY MAYOR FOR SHIT. Every morning, Nat would arrive at City Hall wearing headphones, listening to operas like *Lucia di Lammermoor*. When he took off the headphones, the real-life opera began.

Leventhal was a formidable mixture of intelligence, street smarts, and political savvy. He was also considered by many, including me, to be one of the most effective deputy mayors ever. A bold public servant, Nat made unpopular decisions and solved real problems, including the very toughest. One morning when several of us were meeting with Mayor Koch in his City Hall office, the door flew open and a visibly upset Leventhal shouted at the mayor, "Who the fuck authorized a prison on Staten Island?"

Koch meekly raised his hand and said, "I did."

"Great," Leventhal shouted, "how the hell am I supposed to manage all these programs if you go out and arrange things I don't know about?" Then he left and slammed the door.

We were stunned. But the mayor just shrugged and said, "Oh, don't worry, that's only Nat. It'll be fine. He'll get over it," underscoring the fact that the mayor had a great appreciation for competence and leadership. Leventhal excelled at both.

On the evening we opened three shelters simultaneously, a group of us from HRA, the mayor's office, and Corporation Counsel climbed into a city van to ride around and see how the openings went. Maintaining our policy of keeping shelter sites secret, the drivers of the supply trucks with the beds, mattresses, sheets, pillows, and towels, as well as the buses transporting the homeless, weren't even told their destinations until just before heading out. Local politicians from the communities where the shelters were sited were given only two hours' notice that the homeless were on their way.

The opening in Brooklyn went without incident, as did the one at the Kingsbridge Armory in the Bronx. In Brooklyn, the streets were dark and one man walking his dog came up to us to ask what was going on. When we told him we were opening a shelter, he said, "Oh, that's good." We were pleasantly surprised. The Kingsbridge Armory in the Bronx was the largest armory in the entire country, with six levels below the massive main drill floor filled with tanks and howitzers. Some of the homeless were Vietnam veterans, and our public affairs man, Jack Deacy, imagined a *Daily News* headline: "Homeless Seize Tanks and Howitzers in Bronx and Roll toward Manhattan."

From the Bronx, we headed down to the armory between East 66th and 67th Streets in Manhattan, one of the most exclusive neighborhoods in town. On the way, we took bets as to how long it would take lawyers for the wealthy Upper East Side to drag us into court to block the opening, but I actually believed that wouldn't happen. I felt the 67th Street Armory would be the "guilt" shelter, that the richest community in New York City would willingly do their part. As it turned out, I was right.

When we arrived, the annual black-tie Antiques Show opening was just coming to an end, and hundreds of men in tuxedos and women in gowns were heading for their chauffeur-driven cars as, just around the corner, 100 homeless men trudged up the stairs to their new shelter on the top floor. When they got there, the local councilman, Bob Dreyfus, who'd learned about the shelter just two hours before, was waiting for them, smiling, holding a large bouquet of flowers and offering bowls of fresh fruit. He welcomed the homeless men—noblesse oblige on full, gracious display. When we recovered from the shock, we theorized that liberal New York politics, guilt, and the ubiquitous presence of 24-hour Upper East Side doormen were the reasons we were so well received.

But the welcome didn't last. When we attempted to expand the Park Avenue Armory shelter to house even more people the following winter, State Senator Roy Goodman went ballistic. When he justified his objection, warning about the dangerous juxtaposition of hundreds of National Guard rifles and homeless men, Mayor Koch just mocked him, reminding Goodman that the previous year he'd had no objection when the number of homeless in the armory was just 100. To discourage our expansion plan, the National Guard started stationing big guns on the drill floor. When the new deputy mayor, Stanley Brezenoff, angrily told me to call the New York City Police Department to stop them, I ignored him, not wanting to start some conflict between the police and the military. Goodman did succeed in blocking expansion, but that original Park Avenue shelter has survived for 37 years and today shelters homeless women.

Another of my responsibilities was to be the city's liaison to the New York State National Guard, which operates armories throughout the city and state, and unfortunately, the sound of my voice on the telephone was always met with dread on the other side. Every few months, Governor Mario Cuomo told the National Guard to give us another armory to house more homeless. After a while he didn't even bother to let the National Guard know, so I was usually the person to inform them we'd been granted permission to appropriate another of their armories for a shelter.

Despite this, I developed a very good relationship with General Lawrence Flynn, the second in command of the New York National Guard. Flynn and I both accepted our roles and kept our relations on an even keel. He was a ramrod-straight, decorated US Marine, and one year I watched him lead the Guard as they marched up Fifth Avenue in the St. Patrick's Day parade. Flynn had two Irish wolfhounds, one on either side. I kidded him that even though he was a military man, he was the biggest social worker in New York State in the war against homelessness, and that because of him we sheltered thousands.

One day, Flynn called me to say that he had recently visited the most notorious of the armories—the Fort Washington Armory in Washington Heights, Manhattan. Since we used the enormous drill floor, we were able to house 1,000 men. It was definitely an excessive number of people, but then again, we were in desperate need of beds. Flynn told me that while he had been in four wars and walked amongst his men without worry or fear, visiting this shelter had made him afraid. Many of the men were young and full-bodied, many were addicted, and others had done time at Rikers. It was a really tough crowd, and Flynn told me we had to do something about it. He frightened me, and in response we equipped the site with metal detectors, stepped up security, tightened curfew rules, and were ever more vigilant about bad behavior. Fortunately, things never really got out of hand. After all, shelters were not lockups. People were free to come and go.

We received a lot of criticism for the number of men housed there, and eventually, state regulation limited new shelters to 200 people in any single facility. Bathroom and shower ratios were specified in the consent decree, so we built 100 toilets in that armory at enormous cost. But it was overkill—even at peak times, those toilets were underutilized, which meant installing them had been an unnecessary expenditure. I arranged for a study to prove how wasteful it was. My analysts were not happy, but they did it, and true to our instincts, there actually were far too many toilets. This follows a statistical theory known as queuing theory. If you need 1 toilet for 10 people, you'd think you should keep the ratio of toilets to people consistent as the number of users rises. (So, 10 toilets for 100 people.) But, per queuing theory, you'd actually need a lower ratio of toilets to people as the number of users increased. We proved this in real time with our "toilet study," but Jack Deacy wouldn't let us publish it. He said that even if we were right, the media would make mincemeat out of us. The newspapers found out about it anyway and slammed us for wasting money on a toilet study.

In October 1982, the city requested in court that the highly restrictive plumbing ratios outlined in the consent decree be modified, since they required the city to spend tremendous amounts of money in order to comply. We requested a less onerous provision to meet the needs of the homeless and were amazed that an editorial in the *New York Times*, almost always favorable to the advocates, this time sided with us: "The city's request to modify plumbing ratios in the shelters is not heartless. It is sensible and economically prudent. To oppose sensible changes in the court mandate for toilets and showers is to waste reformist energies." Nevertheless, the court rejected the city's request.

A few months after opening the Fort Washington Armory, we learned that local high schools used the drill floor for track meets. Rather than upset the young runners, we figured out a way to push all the beds to the middle and clear the running track during the day. It worked for a time. But the experience gave us an idea. We decided to have a track meet for our shelter residents . . . but how would we get running sneakers for the team? Then someone had an idea: we went to the Achilles Heel Running Club, and they gave us 500 sneakers from one-legged runners who needed only one shoe per pair. Our staff matched up odd shoes and made pairs for our runners. It was great, and Mayor Koch even presided over an outdoor meet held in Lower Manhattan. Now New York City had the fastest homeless men in the nation! And when we received thousands of knock-off LaCoste polo shirts from a legal settlement, our men were even wearing upscale polos. Now they were not only the fastest, they were also the best dressed. Now and then, we needed light moments like this to keep us sane.

Mayor Ed Koch was not known as a liberal, but he really felt for the homeless. Not only did he sign the groundbreaking consent decree in 1981 out of moral conviction, but he supported the creation of thousands of beds in order to comply. In later years, though, he regretted signing the decree, since it obligated the city to huge and unpredictable expenses. But his act of signing the consent decree was crucial in the annals of American social services in the 20th century. Until that decree was signed, homeless people were viewed as so marginal that even the established social services world didn't want to deal with them. City programs for the mentally ill showed no particular interest in the homeless, and those working with victims of domestic violence set up entirely dedicated shelters so as not to be associated with the homeless population. The Affordable Housing establishment and the New York Housing Authority also shunned them and fought tooth and nail to keep them out.

I always believed the real miracle was that the government of New York City gave us a real budget and genuine political support to provide beds for the homeless. Even more amazing is that we were actually able to provide them. We received endless criticism; still, we provided tens of thousands of homeless men and women (and later, families with children) with a place to sleep and three hot meals a day. No other city in the nation, or perhaps the world, provides the scope of services to the homeless that New York does. Today the city's annual budget for the homeless is well over $1 billion.

We were offered another federal site, an old bachelor officers' quarters at the former Floyd Bennett airfield in Brooklyn. The site was three miles from the nearest residential neighborhood, but still there was a virulent reaction from nearby Marine Park residents. At the community meeting that I attended, there were 400 angry locals hell-bent on blocking the shelter. Tempers boiled over, and we had to be escorted out of the meeting by the NYPD. Yet again, the feds backed off, and that was when we decided to pursue only state- or city-owned sites. It also confirmed that secrecy was our best policy. Though notorious for our "under cover of night" shelter openings, we had no choice. Community protests happened after the fact.

Eventually, our new HRA administrator, Jack Krauskopf, put his foot down on clandestine ops. Krauskopf preferred a gradual approach and decided to give more public notice for a shelter opening in Harlem. We had obtained permission to repurpose an unused public school in the shadow of the old Polo Grounds, where the New York Giants and later the Mets played in central Harlem. The community received a mere two days' notice about the shelter opening, but immediately, hundreds of residents showed up to protest. The protest was huge and angry, and we needed a large police presence to escort about 40 homeless men into the shelter the first night. Threats continued, and the NYPD set up a temporary command center in the shelter for the next few weeks. It did finally calm down, but it was a disaster for community relations. Our original plan to set up in secret seemed a much better idea.

Eventually, new mayors gave even more notice. Still, it was always difficult for a community to accept a shelter in their midst. Yet, in virtually all cases, and despite initial outrage, the shelters became good neighbors, and the communities eventually accepted them. The biggest concern was always safety, and then, of course, the fear that the shelter's presence would decrease property values. In reality, though, that never actually occurred.

A few months after opening the Harlem shelter, we decided to experiment with a voluntary work program. Believing that such a program might engender much-needed motivation for the men as well as pride, we hoped the community would also be pleased, and we designed a program for men to work 20 hours a week cleaning up the neighborhood. In exchange, we gave them a small stipend rather than a salary. We knew that making such a work program mandatory would cause opposition and that the Coalition for the Homeless would probably drag us into court again. The coalition, our constant watchdog, was leery of our work program because they saw shelter as a right, not a privilege. To them, forcing people to work was an impediment to their entitlement to shelter. So, when we introduced the program at the Harlem shelter, we made it abundantly clear that the program was on a voluntary basis and that anyone who chose not to participate could be transferred to another shelter. To our delight, no one opted out. The program was a great success, and the morale of the men improved tremendously. We were watched, but never stopped. Mayor Koch particularly loved this program, since it was consonant with his ethic of personal responsibility.

Every few months someone had the "brilliant" idea to use ships to house the homeless. People who knew nothing about ships and even less about housing the homeless always thought that by floating them on the water and not in a neighborhood, we'd eliminate siting issues. After my experience running the *Gold Star Mother* ferryboat as a methadone clinic in the early '70s, I became the city's resident expert on ships for the homeless, and one day I was summoned to the Housing commissioner's office to meet with yet another donor who wanted us to use his ship for a shelter. The donor was a well-meaning Protestant minister who'd been granted a mothballed troop ship by Congress to be used for charitable purposes. Of course, ships for the homeless was his *great idea*.

I tried to kill it then and there, but the commissioner insisted we take a look. So, we arranged a trip to the James River in Virginia, where hundreds of gray surplus navy ships were mothballed. One hot summer day, I flew with Bob White (our man for shelters) and a fire department deputy commissioner to meet the minister and board the ship. We took a small launch to one of these giant gray ghosts, climbed up the side on a rope ladder, and prepared to inspect. But first, the minister insisted that we pray. We prayed. Then he handed out baloney sandwiches and apples. Was this really happening? Then our inspection began.

The fire department deputy commissioner asked the name of the ship, and when he heard it was the USS *Walker*, he was startled because when he was in the navy, he'd been transported to Korea on that very ship—and had been seasick for the entire two-week journey. The ship was totally unusable for our purposes: low ceilings, structural hurdles every few feet, bunks stacked five high. Maintenance would have been completely prohibitive. We flew back to New York—just another day in the life.

One day, the mayor went to visit the Franklin Avenue Armory shelter in the Bronx at lunchtime. Waiting in line, he asked out loud how the food was. A tall, slender man sashayed up to him and said, "We're having quiche and salad today." The mayor seemed surprised and whispered, "If you feed them like that, they'll never leave." We advised him that lunch was actually franks and beans, and he laughed. Absurdity abounded, and black humor and laughter were necessary to get through the day. A martini or two after work was a big help. . . .

There was always a funny, bizarre tale to be told. One day we heard from the owner of the Palace Hotel, one of the flophouses in the Bowery where we used to pay for homeless men to get a night's sleep. He told us that he'd had a visit from Leona Helmsley's management staff. She had just opened a super-luxurious hotel in Midtown on Madison Avenue just east of St. Patrick's Cathedral. Her hotel was called the Palace, but her European guests complained that when they called to make reservations, they had problems. Helmsley discovered that if you dialed NYC information for the number of the Palace Hotel, the Palace in the Bowery came up first. When guests called and asked the room rates, they were told "two seventy-five" a night, meaning of course $2.75 in the Bowery. Then the conversation got weird when they were told there were no private bathrooms, no views . . . only curfews. Oy.

Helmsley's managers went slumming to ask the hotel owner in the Bowery if he would change the name of his Palace. "No way," he said. "We've been in business for 100 years. You change yours." So the Helmsleys changed the name of their hotel to the Helmsley Palace. Then, Jack Deacy's fake *Daily News* headline was "Bowery Defeats the Billionaire Helmsleys." Both hotels still prevail, but the Helmsley is now owned by a different billionaire, and the flophouse has been renovated and is owned by the Bowery Residents Committee, a nonprofit serving the homeless in NYC.

In winter 1982, the city had no organized program to take homeless people directly off the freezing streets. Rebecca Smith was a 61-year-old African American woman who suffered from schizophrenia and was living on 10th Avenue and 17th Street in Manhattan. She originally came to our attention through neighborhood residents who were concerned for her welfare. For months, HRA tried all kinds of approaches to convince Rebecca to come to a shelter, but time and again she refused.

We discussed the case with Dr. Sara Kellerman, the city's Mental Health commissioner. Kellerman was a believer in the then-popular Thomas Szasz school of thought that mental illness didn't really exist. Szasz believed that there was no mental illness per se, just a society or environment around the person that was unable to recognize or accept different states of reality. (Szasz's theories were briefly popular but eventually faded away.) When we tried to convince Commissioner Kellerman that Rebecca Smith was in danger and urged her to issue an order for Smith to be brought to a hospital, Kellerman refused. Rebecca stayed on the street.

It was late January in the middle of a very cold spell, and the next day we went to a New York State Supreme Court judge for an order to get Ms. Smith off the streets and into a warm shelter. The judge issued the order, but that very night Rebecca Smith froze to death. We were devastated. There was a public outcry, and a prominent TV reporter named Gabe Pressman savagely criticized the city and HRA. Although our staff, the police, and others had made literally dozens of attempts to get Rebecca Smith off the street and out of harm's way, our efforts went largely unreported. It took a *Washington Post* editorial to set the record straight about New York City's ceaseless efforts on Smith's behalf. A few weeks later, Mayor Koch wrote me a personal note thanking me for everything our staff had done.

After the death of Rebecca Smith, Bob Trobe successfully fought for a new law to be passed in Albany, one that could be used to involuntarily hospitalize persons in circumstances of self-harm for a 72-hour medical evaluation. Mayor Koch issued an emergency order called "Code Blue" to authorize the police to bring people to shelters or hospitals when the temperature hit 32 degrees or below. That process is still in effect today and has no doubt saved many lives.

In December 1984, we learned that four staff members at the main East Third Street men's shelter had died of AIDS in the previous six-month period. The AIDS epidemic among gay men and intravenous drug users was just beginning, and little was known or understood about the disease. Bob Trobe and I were terrified that news of these staff deaths would spread panic throughout the homeless population as well as the shelter staff. Rumors about what caused AIDS and how it spread were rampant. I went to the new HRA commissioner, George Gross, and asked him to contact the Health commissioner to request that the Health Department assign a high-level professional to the shelter program to help us determine risks so we could do everything in our power to mitigate them. The Health Department sent several of their top experts to the men's shelter and began holding meetings with the staff and then with shelter residents to explain all that was known at the time. They assured everyone that while there was no need for panic, there was a need for knowledge and prevention techniques. By acting quickly, we were able to avoid rumors and chaos. We called an emergency meeting with leaders of Local 371, the Social Service Employees Union that represented our shelter staff, and laid out all we knew. We explained that we'd enlisted experts from the Health Department to advise and help us. And because we were totally up front with them, the union trusted that we were on the case.

After Ed Koch left office, his successor, David Dinkins, reorganized HRA and created a specialized agency, the Department of Homeless Services. And in 1992, Mayor Dinkins opened the door for nonprofits to operate shelters instead of having the city run them directly. Dinkins's successor, Rudy Giuliani, tried to make the homeless disappear, but he failed miserably. In no way could he reduce the numbers of homeless coming to the city for shelter.

During his first term, Mayor Michael Bloomberg, who promoted the city's economic growth and prosperity, was sure he could solve the problem and promised to reduce the homeless by two-thirds. His staff warned him against making such a claim publicly, but he did. It was a bad move, and regardless of his efforts, the numbers of homeless New Yorkers continued to increase. After a struggle with Governor Andrew Cuomo on the budget, Bloomberg made the catastrophic decision to shut down the city's rent subsidy program, leaving 14,000 families already in their own apartments without money to pay the rent. Consequently, they poured back into the shelters.

Then Bloomberg started blaming the homeless themselves. This was the most stunning public policy mistake I had ever seen. The homeless issue is huge and confounding, not easily "solved." After that decision, the number of people in shelters doubled, and it took years to reestablish a new rent subsidy program.

But by 1992 (long after I left the agency), when then-new Mayor Dinkins began transferring shelter management to private nonprofit agencies and closed almost all the city-operated ones, the profile of a homeless individual had already changed radically. Rather than single men, most of the homeless were families with children. Today, the numbers seeking shelter in NYC continue to rise. By 2018 there were 60,000 people sheltered each night, including 13,000 families with 23,000 children. The turnover or length of stay was roughly 10 months, and there were new people every year.

Homelessness became a major issue in New York City in the '80s and has stayed that way for almost 40 years. And always the numbers go up, with no end in sight due to the structural issues of extremely expensive housing. The overwhelming public perception of homelessness is of the deranged, slovenly, drunk man, or a bag lady carrying all her belongings in a shopping cart and muttering to herself. While these images may be true up to a point, today they are totally inadequate. Today, thousands of families with children are homeless too. While homeless families are rarely seen on the streets of New York, they actually represent two-thirds of the total homeless population. Included are some 23,000 children mostly under the age of 12, with many infants and toddlers.

Homeless families are typically headed by single women who have spent a year or more trying to get help before they actually apply for city shelter. Doubling up in other people's apartments, couch-surfing, and crowding in, they overstay their welcome with family or friends. Homeless families have some common precipitating problems: evictions are the biggest issue, domestic violence another, with mothers fleeing their abusers in the middle of the night. Mental illnesses such as severe depression and anxiety leave families ill-equipped to navigate a harsh city. Serious health issues such as diabetes, autism, and AIDS are also prevalent.

At HRA, Trobe and I sheltered single homeless men and women, but HRA's Crisis Intervention Services division, led by Robert Jorgen, handled displaced families at that time. Jorgen was a former social worker, and his agency specialized in working with families in crisis. Until the 1980s, most of the families they served were made homeless by fires in their buildings. There were a lot of fires in New York, especially in the South Bronx and Brooklyn. CIS rescued burned-out families, putting them up in temporary welfare hotel rooms. But in the 1980s, homeless families began to stream into HRA for many different reasons, and a whole new consent decree was formulated. *McCain v. Koch* was written in 1983 to guarantee shelter for families as well as individuals. HRA also opened five shelters dedicated to battered women. In reality, the majority of families escaping domestic violence were directed to regular family shelters because they guaranteed space.

The city's policies regarding homeless families have evolved decade after decade. In the 1980s, families were sheltered in welfare hotels such as the Martinique in Herald Square, but eventually the hotels became filthy, dangerous places. Then the city began creating communal shelters for families, but these, too, became unmanageable and were riddled with crime and child abuse. There was also a total lack of privacy. Finally, regulated, licensed shelters operated by dedicated nonprofit agencies were established.

Today there are hundreds of nonprofit managed family shelters in the city. Homeless families represent less than 1 percent of households in New York City, and the primary goal for sheltered families is to find permanent housing. And because affordable apartments for even the middle class are virtually nonexistent in NYC, permanent housing for homeless families requires subsidizing their rents. For decades, the city struggled with various rent subsidy programs. Some were successful, but many were not.

While today there's a much more effective funding plan for homeless families, it still takes over a year in the shelter system for a family to capture a decent rent subsidy, find an apartment, and move in. And there's no end in sight, because as one family moves out of a shelter into subsidized housing, another family moves in. I believe that as long as affordable housing is scarce, the city must accept that homeless families will always be with us and that rather than "curing" homelessness, a more realistic solution is to provide subsidies so that those families can live independently. It is an important and, in the end, relatively small financial commitment for a city with a heart as rich and dynamic as New York's.

Providing Home Care

IN 1978 THE ISSUES OF HOMELESSNESS in New York City were about to explode, but it was not the only crisis we faced. The city's home-care program was in deep trouble. It provided government-funded, home-based personal care services for an estimated 10,000 elderly, disabled, and low-income New Yorkers. But since its inception in the late '60s, it had become an administrative disaster. Bob Trobe and I, and the Family and Adult Services staff, were charged with reforming a popular and valuable system that had gone out of control.

Home care, then known as personal care, was a part of Medicaid, the new federal effort to assist low-income elderly and disabled Americans with healthcare, including mental health and long-term nursing care services. It was a part of President Lyndon Johnson's "Great Society" plan for the nation.

Medicaid was designed to give states the flexibility to tailor their own plans and select from several optional services beyond the mandated core services. One option was "personal care," also known as homemaking or housekeeping, which included nonmedical services like meal preparation and assistance with bathing, dressing, shopping, house cleaning . . . essentially all the services that enabled people to remain in their own homes as they aged or became disabled. Very few states selected this personal care option, but New York, with its significantly large aging population, substantial welfare rolls, and growing nursing home program, enthusiastically added it. For one thing, home care was viewed as a less expensive alternative to nursing home care. Best of all, the federal government would pay 50 percent of the cost, with the city and state covering 25 percent each.

Our program, known as the Home Attendant Program, was a welcome addition for all. Home attendants themselves consisted of thousands of female workers, mostly from the Caribbean, who cared for elderly patients at home. The system was set up as quickly as possible because need for it was tremendous, and because the administrators believed the program could save the city and state a great deal of money.

Most seniors prefer to stay in their own homes as they age. Regardless of their disability, the desire to stay home rather than enter a nursing home is the choice of almost everybody. Usually, whether someone goes to a nursing home or stays in their own home toward the end of their life depends on whether they have a daughter living close by, since daughters are far more likely than sons to help care for aging parents. Also, the cost of nursing homes can be prohibitive. It is funded by Medicaid for the indigent poor, but many middle-class people run out of money while they are in their own homes before they can qualify for Medicaid.

While most states do not use Medicaid for funding home care, in New York State the government chose to utilize Medicaid for long-term home care in addition to nursing homes. As a result, there are now fewer nursing homes per capita in New York than in other states, a positive result.

Home care can be as little as a few hours a week to 24 hours a day for each client. Even with more hours, for a single person it is still less expensive than a nursing home. Ironically, even if home care were not funded by the government, many people in the community would still choose not to go to a nursing home regardless of how badly they need care. Now, with home care as an option, many more people receive some kind of government-reimbursed care. Today, the budget for home care in New York is quite large and equal to that for nursing homes.

In 1978 home attendant jobs were poorly paid, with the aides making the existing minimum wage of $3.35 an hour without any health insurance, sick pay, or other benefits. They were underpaid, unsung heroes who, despite their own hardships, were often exceptionally devoted to those they cared for. And the city lived up to the adage that no good deed goes unpunished, because not only were aides poorly paid, they were not even paid on time. Often their pay-checks were three to four months behind, but they still showed up to care for their patients.

Home health aides were considered "independent contractors" hired by patients. The aides' murky status was much like that of the "gig" or freelance workers of today. In order for the city to have some semblance of control, their paychecks had to be signed by both pa-tient and caregiver. It was a clumsy, unsustainable process, yet the terrible delays in getting home attendants paid turned out to be just the tip of the iceberg of a massively dysfunctional program inundat-ed with complaints and widely criticized by all.

There were also long delays in securing approval for those who needed home care. Hundreds of records were lost or incomplete, and computer systems collapsed on a regular basis. Administrators, so-cial workers, patients, attendants, doctors, and families had no idea where to turn for help, and slinging blame was endless. Confusion and frustration reigned. Many had tried and failed to solve these problems, and now it was our turn. Bob Trobe and I worked togeth-er to divvy up the myriad tasks of our complicated division, each of us relying on our particular strengths. Trobe and I trusted each oth-er; we each knew exactly what we were doing, and we assigned re-sponsibilities and tasks within FAS to try to accomplish even more.

The Home Attendant Program was financed by Medicaid and cared for 10,000 people. I designed and executed a unique financial structure, as well as the whole contracting process from requests for proposal to selection, to opening new nonprofits. I also worked with the New York State regulators. Before I arrived, Trobe had al-ready begun to tackle the most urgent part of the problem, getting the aides paid. He hired Greg Kaladjian, a smart and driven man-ager, to focus entirely on the payment system. Kaladjian brought on staff to construct and maintain a reliable database and create and monitor an efficient paper-flow system. He discovered that hundreds of records were incomplete or lost because the existing computer system frequently collapsed. He created the term *NIF*. *NIF* meant *not in files*, meaning they'd looked for a person's record

As we saw it, there were two options for restructuring. The first was to have the city itself hire aides as civil servants. The second was to spin the caseload out to private nonprofit agencies. We decided on the second option, which would generate dozens of private, nonprofit agencies to supervise smaller clusters of caseloads. Making home health aides city employees would have meant adding extensive fringe benefits and costly, rigid civil service rules for thousands, a financial commitment we wanted to avoid. District Council 37, which represented social service workers, was already planning to unionize home attendants, forcing our hand to accept the cumbersome and expensive first option. Had DC 37 succeeded in getting home health aides classified as city employees, the program cost would have tripled and made day-to-day management prohibitive. Through nonprofits, aides could be managed locally throughout city neighborhoods. This would create more personalized service whereby administrators knew both clients and aides, *and* the program could be managed at a significantly lower cost.

I assumed responsibility for designing a contracting system that would divide caseloads into smaller quantities in order to make them more manageable for not-for-profit agencies. Hardly any of the existing larger agencies could handle a caseload of thousands, so we created a new "paint by numbers" system. We laid out blueprints that could be used for bidding and selecting existing and new nonprofits.

We were concerned that some agencies might have reporting problems, so we also designed and centralized information systems and developed an unusual financing plan to ensure that a half billion dollars could not be misappropriated. Designing that system took us another year. We wrote an innovative contract that separated administrative costs from the payroll. A customized computer system would track hours of care and match them with the payroll, and we worked with an expert software developer to fashion a well-vetted program that all nonprofit agencies could access and use. Through the use of a single system, actual payroll money could be monitored. Agencies would report the hours for each aide, and a dedicated computer service would match them against the city's authorization and then run the paychecks. All other administrative functions would be defined in more than once and never found it. He created a systematized feed-back report to retrieve missing client information from hundreds of individual social workers in another part of HRA (known as GSS—General Social Services) to redeem the lost material. The GSS workers were frustrated because while they tried to get the program applications in, they, too, were repeatedly foiled by lost data. Finger pointing was epidemic.

We set up a task force between Greg's operation and the so-cial-worker division to coordinate and track information. Bobbi Poussaint and Nick Borg headed the GSS division, and Ken Klug, a bright, knowledgeable, yet understated civil servant, worked closely with Greg and staff on both sides to try to straighten it out. It took six months of incredible diligence and focus, but eventually workers were paid on time and data flowed reasonably well.

I observed Greg's management techniques, a tracking plan for task analysis that detailed every step of the process and assigned specific staff to each one. With Greg's plan, everyone knew their re-sponsibility, as well as everyone else's. He conducted regular updates where certainly no one wanted to admit they hadn't done their part. I used that technique of accountability for decades, and it worked remarkably well.

In 1979 HRA commissioner Stanley Brezenoff declared that virtually all of the major payroll challenges of the existing Home Attendant Program had been resolved. It was true that part of the problem had indeed been resolved, but plenty of other critical issues remained. A major one was the need to restructure the entire system in order to comply with state and federal labor laws and to estab-lish reasonable supervision of thousands of aides and clients. For years, aides and clients were left entirely on their own. That meant that neither had anywhere to turn for substitutes, replacements, or other problems. No one was reporting earnings to the IRS, and no one was paying taxes. Maintaining the fiction of "independent con-tractors" was legally unsustainable. (Many of those problems mirror those we have today in the ever-increasing gig economy.) Several at-tempts at reforming this ill-managed program had failed, and every-body believed we'd fail too.

great detail in the contracts themselves, and line-item budgets were established to make sure contractors were paid only for necessities: nurses, coordinators (the supervisors of home-care workers), office space, computer services, telephone, and liability insurance.

Utilizing everything I'd learned at the Health Department while opening contracted methadone clinics, we convinced HRA lawyers to compose a detailed contract specifying each and every step not-for-profits had to take. It was their first contract that incorporated such rules. The agencies had to ensure that employees met legal standards for hiring and HRA reserved the right to prescribe experience requirements for all office staff as well as aides, and to review and approve of every prospective program administrator new contractors hoped to hire.

Because all previous efforts at reform had failed, dozens of stakeholders watched our every move. We knew we had to convince all parties involved that we were listening to their ideas, and we had many conversations with prominent social service entities like Catholic Charities, the United Jewish Appeal, and the Federation of Protestant Agencies, as well as the city's Department for the Aging and the state Department of Health. We also met with various think tanks such as the United Hospital Fund and the Brookdale Center in addition to several home healthcare associations. By listening, we learned. There was enormous interest in this program, along with great skepticism that it could be reformed. The huge numbers of patients and attendants and the amount of money involved generated a great deal of interest and gave cause for no small amount of anxiety.

After writing the contract requirements, we circulated them widely and then held a major conference with potential nonprofit bidders. The first conference lasted hours and hours. We went through every line of the contract and recorded all comments. We responded to each point in writing and as a result made a few changes in the contract language. At a second conference, we listened to comments and answered questions. Everyone knew what was expected of them, and by being totally transparent, we achieved buy-in from all parties.

The next step in the reform began when we put the home-care proposal out for bid. The response was overwhelming, and we received more than 60 proposals from nonprofit agencies that wanted to be a part of this new, efficient, and workable home-care system. We set up bid review teams at HRA so that multiple readers reviewed and rated each nonprofit agency proposal. We had an elaborate rating system for each bidder, including their written plans and their track record for financial responsibility and performance history. Then we rated the proposals and decided how many patients—from 200 to 1,000—to assign each contractor.

It was critical for us to avoid any outside influence in the selection process, and we needed the solid support of the mayor. There were many in the nonprofit community who wanted their agency to be awarded a contract, and they applied plenty of lobbying and political pressure. But we maintained our process. Our transparency and the support of the mayor won the day. Once we were directed to take a lunch meeting with Stanley Friedman, a well-known and powerful local political boss, to describe our contracting process. Friedman quickly understood that we were not going to be influenced by outsiders and said, "I get that you're avoiding political influence, but do you have to reward even the mayor's enemies?"

In the midst of our Herculean effort to transform the system, there was one interest group that was totally opposed to the idea of reform. A small but very militant group wanted to scuttle the entire effort. The severely disabled quadriplegic activists were probably less than 3 percent of patients, but we immediately understood that they needed to approve of our plan. In their view, the home-care program was tied to their very existence. The Quads (their name for themselves) opposed our reform because it threatened the freedom and control of the original program. We knew they could stop us cold by influencing city politicians and enlisting the press for support. The potential spectacle of quadriplegics circling their wheelchairs around City Hall and stopping traffic on the Brooklyn Bridge was not lost on us, so we set up a special task force to address their concerns.

The Quads

I T WAS MONDAY, AUGUST 7, 1978. I had a roomy, sunny corner office on the 13th floor at headquarters. (The 13th floor must have been an omen.) My boss, Bob Trobe, was out for the day, and on his schedule was a late-morning meeting with Commissioner Blanche Bernstein in the 15th-floor conference room. Trobe's calendar notes read, "11 a.m.: Commissioner's meeting re: home care/ Quads." Quads? I went upstairs to represent him at the meeting. When the elevator door opened on the 15th floor, two wheelchairs rolled ahead of me toward the conference room with two middle-aged women quadriplegics breathing through tubes attached to small oxygen tanks. They were accompanied by their aides, the women who helped make their lives livable.

When we arrived, you could feel the tension in the air. I took a seat at the head of a long conference table and was soon surrounded by 10 angry quadriplegics. Several other HRA officials I did not yet know joined us, and I introduced myself.

When everyone had arrived, Commissioner Bernstein came in. Dr. Bernstein, an economist, was a short, rather formal and severe older woman who smoked cigarettes in a long silver holder, in bizarre contrast to the Quads (which, once again, is what they called themselves) in wheelchairs. Bernstein had broken through the glass social services ceiling to become the first woman HRA commissioner, and the fact that the Human Resources Administration had been a man's world was evidenced on the conference room walls displaying photographs of 18 previous HRA and Department of Welfare commissioners.

In the room, there was considerable fiddling with electrical equipment and wheelchair repositioning, and there was the constant whirring of breathing apparatuses. The commissioner welcomed everyone and acknowledged that the Quads were here because they had objected to proposed home-care changes that the city planned to adopt later in the year. But a spokeswoman for the Quad group quickly interrupted her.

"Excuse me, Commissioner, let's make ourselves clear at the outset." The speaker, a woman, talked in a staccato voice and was able to say only a few words before turning her head to take another breath of oxygen. "Your new home-care plan is totally unacceptable to us. For us, it represents a return to the days when we were institutionalized, stuck in hospitals and nursing homes. We fought for over a decade to be able to live independent lives, to really live! And we are never going back."

The message was clear. The other Quads shouted in agreement. "Never!" one shouted. "Never going back!" They were angry and agitated. The institutions where they'd felt helpless and trapped for so many years had radicalized them forever.

"And, Commissioner, let me tell you that we will do anything and everything to fight and overturn your plans. Sit-ins, picket lines, civil disobedience, whatever it takes. You better get ready."

Bernstein assured them that she'd gotten their message and said she would set up a special task force that would include them, to see if we could find a solution. "And Bonnie Stone will represent HRA," she announced, pointing at me. I swallowed hard and nodded. The meeting was over. The Quads slowly rolled down the hallway to the elevators.

Over the next 18 months, I would work with these vehement activists in their ultimate civil rights struggle. Working with them would change how I looked at the world forever. From then on, I understood the enormous struggles people who were "different" had to mount in order to be treated with dignity. We didn't know their exact numbers citywide, but it was clear to us that the Quads had the political and emotional capacity to shut down our entire home-care reform effort if we didn't successfully address their concerns. They tended to be decades younger than most home-care clients and had been truly radicalized by their experiences in institutions and nursing homes. They had escaped through organizing, through political pressure, and by taking advantage of the new Medicaid-supported home-care funding, which enabled them to live in their own homes.

I had but a brief month to consider the issues before our negotiations began. One problem was that the Quads viewed "vendorization," the term used to describe the city's transfer of the larger home-care system to nonprofit, contracted agencies, as an existential threat to their independence. If new agencies hired, fired, and paid home attendants, the Quads believed they'd lose the little control they had to direct their care. Some remote bureaucrat would hire, recruit, and schedule aides who would then be working for the agency and not the client. Quads might still be living in their homes, but they would be at the mercy of others who'd control their liberty by taking personal supervision and control of aides out of their hands and placing it in the hands of a remote corporate entity. Taking away that control was a threat to their very existence.

I began our first task force meeting by acknowledging their total objection to our plan. Then I explained the problems we had with keeping the current system. For one thing, according to all labor laws, the system was illegal: no one paid taxes, there were no employee benefits for aides, and there was no insurance of any kind for anyone. Under the current system, there were huge problems in getting aides paid for their work. Also, in order to keep the Medicaid money flowing, we had to meet New York State's regulations that aides be well trained and instructed. And we were racing against the clock, since DC 37, the social services union, was intent on organizing the workforce and challenging the city to convert all the home-care workers into city employees. That outcome was a problem for both sides. For the city, it would more than triple the cost of an already-expensive program; and the Quads, in turn, would completely lose all the personal control they so desperately wanted to preserve. And the idea of having the city manage 10,000 new city employees with individual work schedules and rigid civil service rules in the individual homes of 10,000 vulnerable home-care clients would present a new and even greater nightmare. My goal for the Quad task force was to create a system that solved both our problems and theirs. I was open to their ideas. They were skeptical, of course, but the conversation began. About 45 minutes into the meeting, we adjourned. I asked them to come back the following month with ideas for a solution.

There were three leaders who were the most active in all our negotiations. Sandra Schnur had been totally paralyzed by polio from the neck down since the age of 15. She'd lived for several years in an iron lung, and her doctors had wanted her confined to long-term hospitalization. Sandra had also spent time in Warm Springs, Georgia, at the Institute for Rehabilitation that President Roosevelt, himself a paraplegic, had established in the 1930s. Over the years, the iron lung was replaced with smaller and more manageable breathing apparatuses. Through modern technology, they'd become portable enough for patients to be able to carry them on their wheelchairs and move around more freely.

Sandra was intent on getting an education, joining the outside world, and living independently. She was attractive and well dressed. Her hair was perfectly coiffed, her nails were perfectly polished, and she was extremely well spoken. Sandra married and eventually received a bachelor's and a master's degree. She worked for the mayor's Office for the Handicapped, administering the half-fare program for the disabled.

Over many months, Sandra and I became quite close. I remember one incident when her aide accidentally almost dropped her from her wheelchair as they were getting off the elevator. Sandra quipped, "Just don't drop me on my head, it's the only thing I have that works!"

Once, when we were talking, she said, "Can you imagine how terrible it is to have to wait for someone to bathe and feed and dress you and comb your hair all the time?"

I said, "I don't know, there are many times it sounds absolutely wonderful to me to be waited on totally." Sandra winced. Was I mocking her? What did I mean?

Quickly, I explained, "Sandra, there's no way in the world I could put myself in your shoes and truly understand what you have to deal with. We have had totally different experiences and I respect that, but I could never fully understand your life."

She pondered for a while. "You're right," she said. "Our job is to respect one another, not to try to remake the other in our image." We became even closer. Sandra lived for many more years and died of melanoma in 1994 at the age of 59.

Another leader was Ira Holland, a handsome young man with a slight build and a charming sense of humor. Ira had also suffered from polio since the age of 15 and had been hospitalized on and off for 20 years. He'd spent some time at home with his parents, but they had a hard time coping with his disability. He told me that in his parents' house he'd often thought about suicide and once even tried to starve himself to death. Finally, he moved back to the hospital, where he teamed up with a group of other young Quads and became an activist for the disabled. With the help of his wife, Victoria, and his close friend, Ed Lichter, Ira founded an initiative to support home-care services as a vehicle for independent living. His organization, Concepts of Independence, would be wildly successful for the next four decades. Hundreds of people, including Ira and his wife, were able to live independently because of it. Ira and Victoria had an apartment on Roosevelt Island where they lived out their lives.

In a later conversation, Ira told me that the reason the group was able to negotiate with me was that I didn't "social-work them to death." I told him that on the contrary, I totally recognized their power in this and considered them formidable adversaries and not "patients" at all. "That's why we trusted you," he said.

After we had sealed the deal, Ira brought us a gift of perfume. And although city employees were prohibited from accepting any gifts, we broke the rules and graciously accepted this one. Ira had regained his life after he began to organize his fellow patients at Goldwater Hospital more than 30 years before. He later wrote: "Don't sit and wait for the magic cure to come by, busy yourself, devote yourself, and take advantage of the many miraculous changes that have enabled us to go forward." Victoria predeceased Ira, who died at age 64, at home with his home-care attendants around him.

Another leading activist was Marilyn Saviola, who was somewhat younger and very militant. Marilyn went on to live a long life. When she passed away in December 2019 at age 74, her life was described in an extraordinary *New York Times* obituary. She, too, had spent time hospitalized at Goldwater on Roosevelt Island. She was very skeptical and politically active, and trusted no one. Marilyn, heavyset and somewhat disheveled, had to breathe through an oxygen tube, stopping for a breath after every few words. She was a formidable, unrelenting advocate. Her view was that people saw the severely disabled as either "helpless children" or "sexless throwaways." Women, in particular, were totally invisible and not viewed as whole people. It was not lost on her that returning disabled veterans seemed to be much more respected, even though they, too, had to fight for their rights.

There was no crossing Marilyn, and she went on to become an effective advocate for civil rights for women, healthcare for women and the disabled, and many other causes. Her reputation both locally and nationally continued for four decades. She spent much of her time testifying and speaking about the rights of women and the disadvantaged. She ultimately became the executive director of the Center for Independent Living. In 2018 Marilyn received the Viscardi Award, a national honor for her services.

Over the next 18 months, we laboriously pondered and critiqued each idea the Quads brought us. My executive assistant, Kathy Ruby, a very savvy and experienced person, took careful notes at the meetings. But before each one she'd beg me to let her skip it, because the sight of so many disabled people being hostile toward us was too emotional for her. But I needed a steady hand as witness and coordinator, and Kathy stayed with it to the end. Each meeting was an ordeal for the participants, since each person needed their own ambulette with full services to bring them to HRA headquarters in Manhattan. It meant enormous personal coordination for each participant, but they were all present. I maintained a cool and serious exterior and was able to quietly absorb the group's anger.

I never offered a plan of my own but waited for them to propose something, and then we would sit together and analyze it. Their first proposal was to issue city-generated vouchers to each patient for the services they required. They could then use the money to pay the home-care workers they themselves had hired. It sounded good, but going through all the issues they would have to manage—taxes, fringe benefits, insurance, training, etc.—their voucher proposal was clearly too difficult to implement.

At one point, a pro bono attorney joined them at a meeting, and when he started to cantankerously dominate the conversation, I exploded with mock anger. "I thought we were working together to solve problems," I said. "If you add a lawyer, then I'll have to add lawyers too. Soon we'll have a room full of lawyers arguing amongst themselves, and our chances of coming to an agreement will diminish." I packed up my notes and walked out. I went back to my office, and within a half hour, Sandra Schnur and Ira Holland showed up. We hashed things out for an hour, and I kept to my point that I didn't want a circus, I just wanted to solve problems. I said that if things broke down in the future, there would always be time for lawyers, lawsuits, and protests. They said they'd discuss it and a few days later agreed to monthly meetings, sans lawyers.

After months of exploring several different proposals and making some progress, the Quads came up with a proposal that seemed to meet all their requirements as well as ours. The plan was for them to set up their own nonprofit agency to address the administrative work of payroll, insurance, and so on. Concepts of Independence, the nonprofit created by Ira and Victoria Holland and Ed Lichter, would manage the business side: payroll, billing, fringe benefits, insurance, and so on. The clients themselves would be responsible for recruitment, hiring, replacements, scheduling, supervision, and training of the aides. The only stumbling block was getting the state Department of Social Services to waive state regulations for the training of aides, but we agreed to present the Quads' proposal to the state. After initial skepticism, the state agreed to changes in the training protocols, and at last we had a deal that would allow us to proceed with the larger home-care program conversion for 10,000 elderly New Yorkers. And it was none too soon, because we were racing against the clock before the union locked us all into a rigid and expensive system of city-employed home attendants.

We couldn't discriminate among clients interested in this special program, so we designed an intricate application that let anyone apply and explain how they would manage their responsibilities. Clients would have to write out their own plans for managing their aides. Of course, someone else wrote the document, but under the client's personal direction. The first wave of applications included about 250 people. There was some pushback, since the activists were afraid that once again "ice-cold bureaucrats" would have too much power over them. We realized that anyone who'd go to the trouble of making an application was likely to be accepted, and generally, they were. Today, almost 40 years later, the number of people in this program has grown to 1,000, and the model we established has been incorporated into the statewide home-care program.

So, what did I learn from negotiating with the Quads? First, I learned you have to evaluate your opponent; understand their motivations. What does your opponent really want from the negotiations? What do you need? Second, I learned how crucial it is to understand your opponent's strengths and weaknesses. Third, if at all possible, it is strategic to refrain from promoting your particular idea or position until your opponent presents theirs. By rethinking the Quads as actual partners in problem solving instead of considering them opponents, we were able to craft a plan that truly worked for both sides.

I believe I understood the Quads' point of view, understood their needs as well as any able-bodied person could. Above all, I respected them, their experiences, and their deeply held values. But the bigger lesson was a spiritual one. Here were 10 quadriplegic leaders unable to control much of their lives. They were totally dependent on technology, on the service and kindness of others. Every task—eating, toileting, bathing, dressing, traveling—was an ordeal. Their bodies were virtually useless, and the sum total of their power was in their heads—their brains and their ability to communicate. The Quads willed themselves into living full lives.

Thinking of this many decades later, I remember a childhood neighbor, Leonard Eaton, who had a severe case of cerebral palsy. It was the late 1940s, and Leonard was a few years older than me. All his doctors recommended that Leonard be institutionalized for the long term, but his mother refused. Instead, she kept him home and made certain that he was educated and integrated into our community. In spring and summer, while the rest of us cavorted in the Brooklyn streets, Leonard tracked all the radio stations at once to monitor the various baseball scores, and we'd run into his first-floor apartment every 15 minutes to get the latest scores. All of us were Brooklyn Dodgers fans, but we also had to know how the Yankees and the Giants were doing.

Leonard went on to college, then law school, then got married and had two children. His mother, Nina, played a major role in the founding of the United Cerebral Palsy organization. Leonard lived a full life and died at age 75 in 2017.

I also remember being in California in the late 1970s and watching extremely disabled children being escorted through Disneyland in their wheelchairs and beds. It was thrilling to me. Perhaps those original experiences helped me work with the Quads so many years later.

So, in 1980 we were poised to award contracts ranging from $2 million to $10 million to 45 nonprofit social service agencies that would manage the home-care system. Contract awards passed the Board of Estimate unanimously on a single day. One of them was a special contract for quadriplegics. The full program totaled half a billion annually, yet because of our entirely transparent public process, the members of the Board of Estimate did not challenge any of the contracts, an extraordinary occurrence. I was too busy with my next problem to witness the big vote. But when I heard about the joyful scene and all the crying over our triumph, I regretted missing the moment.

And so began a whole new era in home care. It took a year to transfer all the clients to the various contract agencies, but, all things considered, the process went smoothly. And, as is the case with so many successful government initiatives, we got very little credit. Even one of our chief skeptics in the New York State Department of Social Services, Ann Hallock, agreed that we had really done it. Our reform worked.

I had brought over one of my methadone colleagues to HRA to assist in the Home Attendant Program reform. Maurice Battle, whom I'd worked with in the methadone program, knew a lot about the community. His new boss, Bob Shick, who supervised new contracts, told me that Maurice had once spent 12 hours at his desk processing dozens of staff for the new agencies. "He didn't even take a bathroom break." I was not surprised. Maurice and I had become fast friends, and I knew he was a workaholic. Sadly, only a few years later, Maurice was the first of many colleagues to die of AIDS.

Ten years after home-care reform, I would experience the benefits very personally. In 1979, my father had a major stroke that left him seriously disabled. My mother was able to take care of him for a few years, but after a while their savings were depleted and she was increasingly unable to accomplish the difficult tasks necessary to care for him. After he suffered a fall, a broken hip, and a few months in a nursing home, we applied to HRA for Medicaid home care. Since my parents' Social Security benefits were higher than the minimum, they paid a steep co-pay each month, but it was worth it. My father received 24-hour city home care for several years until his death in 1991. His aide stayed all day to walk him, bathe him, and transfer him from bed to chair, relieving my elderly mom. The aide was a young, effervescent Caribbean woman who made the last years of my father's life completely comfortable at home. The city system we had built years before was everything my family could have wished for.

Forty years later, the same Home Attendant Program is still up and running. It more than tripled in size, and fortunately there were no serious scandals. Very little money was lost to corruption, and tens of thousands of New Yorkers received vital care. Years ago, one contract group finagled a scheme to siphon money from insurance fee kickbacks, but the scam was discovered, the city was reimbursed $400,000, and the contract administrator went to jail. In 2017 our reformed Home Attendant Program was integrated into the New York State Long Term Care Program, which includes nursing homes and skilled home-care nursing.

In 2010 Bob Trobe and I were honored at the anniversary of Concepts of Independence, Inc. Though most of the folks who worked on the original plan were gone, Bob and I were designated "the mother and father of Concepts of Independence" and were showered with appreciation.

The Americans with Disabilities Act was finally signed by Congress in 1990. Across the nation, before and after the new act, there was considerable hostility toward making serious accommodations for the disabled. Businesses, even churches, joined the opposition, claiming that the extreme costs of physical rebuilding were prohibitive. For transportation systems, accommodating wheelchairs was considered preposterous. The general attitude was *these people aren't worth it*, and it wasn't until disabled young veterans returning from Vietnam took up the cause that the idea of accommodating the disabled really took hold. And of course, all the activism around this issue originated in New York City.

Keepers of the Flame

OTHER, SMALLER PROGRAMS were under our charge at HRA: senior citizens' centers, family planning, protective services for adults, adult homes, and all other programs for adults except income maintenance. It was fantastic working with Bob Trobe. I was his deputy for six years, and together we tackled some huge and intractable problems. From the first day of negotiating with the Quads to the signing of that 1981 consent decree, we worked ourselves to the bone. Each morning, reading the newspapers, I could see how the agency was part of the very pulse of New York City life. HRA was the keeper of the flame of all social policy. We received enormous criticism and got very little credit, and yet we truly did serve the people.

Gallows humor often saved us, and once, Jack Deacy, our deputy commissioner for Public Affairs, was in a meeting discussing the mandatory release of a report on children who'd died while in the custody of HRA. The City Council required that we report this after the particularly gruesome deaths of a few children who'd been involved in Special Services, and to put it mildly, we were expecting a very bad response from the press. But during a break in the meeting, somebody whispered to Jack that the *Challenger* space shuttle had just exploded, killing all the astronauts. So when Jack returned to the meeting, he suggested that they get their grim report out "immediately," in the futile hope that the *Challenger* disaster would overshadow the HRA death march. It was, indeed, callous; still, everyone burst out laughing.

Most days, bad news from HRA overshadowed bad news from any other city agency, and Jack's name was so ubiquitous as HRA's spokesman for some horrible story that people thought he was a made-up person. When Indira Gandhi was assassinated by two Sikhs, I playfully called Lilliam Barrios-Paoli, deputy commissioner for Children's Services, to tell her that the two Sikhs who murdered Gandhi had been in HRA foster care just a couple of years before. Her heart sank. "Oh no, not us again!" I was kidding, but she believed me because no matter what it was, HRA always took the blame. We'd all become absurdist. Lilliam went on to become a deputy mayor under de Blasio.

There were other smaller but still very significant HRA programs. Jimmy LeBosco, a quiet, sad-faced social worker who, like Nat Leventhal, was also an opera buff, headed the program Protective Services for Adults. This was one of the lower-profile HRA programs that worked with the most vulnerable people in the city. Mostly hidden, largely unknown, these were people often characterized as the "craziest folks in town." They were on our radar for assistance only if they lived alone in the community, adamantly refused help, and denied having any problems at all. Worried neighbors or the police usually referred them, and each and every one who was referred tended to have unique, frequently bizarre issues.

One case involved a 50-year-old woman in an apartment in an affluent area on the Upper West Side who lived alone after the death of her parents. She was known as the Pigeon Lady because over the years, she'd knocked out her windows so that hundreds of pigeons, her "children," lived in the apartment with her. The neighbors and the landlord genuinely liked her, but the smell and the health hazard to the Pigeon Lady and her neighbors was considerable. She rejected all visitors, including our social workers, who attempted to bring her food and to have her apartment cleaned. When Bob Trobe and I visited her with her caseworker, the Pigeon Lady immediately fixated on Bob, telling him how "they" had placed electronic implants in her brain. The three of us kept quiet and just listened.

Finally, her landlord was left with no alternative. He moved to evict her, and the case landed in court. Present were her legal aid attorney, an official from Animal Affairs in the Health Department, our Protective Services staff, and the landlord. When the woman's attorney asked if pigeon droppings were poisonous, the health official answered, "Only if disturbed and ingested." He informed us that any cleanup crew would have to wear an oxygen suit that rented for $125 an hour. The woman's attorney asked if the chemicals used to clean up the pigeon droppings were poisonous and would be harmful to the live pigeons too. When the response was affirmative, the judge mused that maybe the pigeons could be suited up as well. In the end, the court ordered a cleanup, the pigeons did not get their own oxygen suits, and the Upper West Side's notorious Pigeon Lady was miraculously able to remain in her apartment.

A Brooklyn woman was convinced that an earthquake occurred in her apartment every single night, and every afternoon she'd pack up her dishes to protect them from the impending quake. Concerned neighbors called HRA. Social workers visited and discovered that the Earthquake Lady was not all that unreasonable, since the nighttime rumbles came from the elevated subway nearby.

Another woman lived in an apartment with nothing but a bed frame, a wooden chair, and a single lightbulb. She left her apartment every day and was given a bagel and coffee by the owner of the corner deli. She was skin and bones. Our social workers checked in with her frequently to get her better food and services.

Sad-eyed Jimmy, the director of Protective Services, lived and breathed this bizarrely depressing world every day. Yet Jimmy really lived for the opera and traveled around the world to performances. At the very mention of opera his face lit up, and Jimmy transformed from sad to joyful.

Working with this vulnerable population, we frequently tried to enlist the assistance of the city's commissioner of Mental Health, Dr. Sara Kellerman. Dr. Kellerman had statutory authority to involuntarily hospitalize people considered dangerous to themselves or to others. But Kellerman, as mentioned earlier, was an adherent of Thomas Szasz's theory that mental illness didn't really exist. By her lights, these folks simply lived in an alternative reality. Thomas Szasz was a famous, often despised psychiatrist who'd published a book claiming that mental illness was a myth. In fairness, he was partially reacting to communist regimes that manipulated psychiatry in order to lock up dissenters.

But at HRA, we regularly saw people in tremendous distress who desperately needed help. Dr. Kellerman repeatedly turned down our requests to hospitalize disturbed and dangerous people in our care, even those with guns. Her views annoyed me, and at interagency meetings, I was so outspoken and almost nasty to her that at one point Stan Brezenoff barred me from attending. He was trying to work with Kellerman, but I found her stance unconscionable in the face of real dangers our staff faced almost daily when dealing with clients who were also a great danger to themselves. Fortunately, Dr. Szasz and his theories have been largely forgotten.

Bob Trobe worked closely with LeBosco on all these special cases of people endangered in their own homes. Trobe believed the city needed a new approach to the problem, and, with Ed Djowski, he designed and implemented a new state regulation allowing nonprofits to apply to become community guardians. For many older people, the court appointed guardians from a roster of attorneys paid out of those people's assets, but generally our folk had so few assets, a private attorney wouldn't take them on. Trobe and Djowski's new regulation enabled the HRA commissioner to contract and pay a qualifying nonprofit to serve as a guardian. Their design was widely implemented and has since become bedrock for all.

Another smaller program oversaw 10 local community Family Planning Clinics that were performing poorly. Trobe engaged Al Moran, the respected executive director of Planned Parenthood, to evaluate them for us. Moran recommended that we create a single, well-staffed nonprofit in order to provide higher-quality services. We agreed, and I began negotiations with the 10 nonprofits to relinquish their charters and join together for a larger, better-funded, and better-functioning agency. The discussions began with great suspicion, but after a while, one sophisticated board member, Will Innis, from a group on Staten Island, saw the light. He and I went to work, and eventually they all agreed to form a single agency.

Now the challenge was to obtain a New York State license for this new entity. We made the application and were bounced around and around by the regulatory staff in an impossible bureaucratic loop. Finally, I realized that normal processes wouldn't work, that I needed another approach. Time was limited, as a $750,000 grant was waiting for our reorganization to be completed. I called on Reuven Savitz, the most sophisticated actor I knew. He was a deputy commissioner at HRA, and I asked him to reach out to the Public Health Council and plead our case. Savitz said he'd love to help, but the fellow in charge of the council was an old enemy. Desperate, I made a cold call to Mort Hyman, chairman of the council, who by luck happened to pick up the phone. I pleaded my case. Hyman didn't know me at all, but after 15 minutes, he said, "Got it. I'll push it through." And he did. We got the license; we got the grant. And what could have died a long, slow death on the bureaucratic vine flourished instead.

In 1981, when we created the Community Family Planning Corporation to run the 10 clinics, I asked Norman Haffner, an old friend and prominent State University of New York deputy chancellor of health, to chair it. Haffner made the clinics a real force for good, and over the years, the clinic program grew and grew. Eventually, Catherine Abate, a former New York state senator, ran it as Community Healthcare Network, and in an ironic twist, since 2014 it has been run by Robert Hayes, the dynamic young lawyer who sued New York City in 1979 on behalf of the homeless.

When Bob Trobe left HRA to become deputy commissioner at the Housing Preservation Department, I took over his job. In 1985 the city initiated yet another reorganization of HRA after recommendations by the new Beattie Commission, formed by Mayor Koch. I believed, quite cynically, that they shook up the agency every few years in the hope that some of the programs would fall off and disappear. I remember one executive meeting in the HRA commissioner's office about reorganizing the various HRA departments and services. Herb Rosenzweig, the legendary deputy administrator for Income Maintenance (welfare payments), was fidgeting. He accidentally broke a pencil, which made a loud cracking sound. The commissioner turned to him and asked if he had something to contribute. "Yes," Herb said, "it strikes me that any way you stack the turds, it's still a pile of shit." Dark humor for sure, but I couldn't have agreed more. Reorganization was a substitute for real problem solving. Just shuffling the deck was a waste of time.

After George Gross took over as commissioner, a terrible incident occurred in which an NYPD officer shot and killed an old woman named Eleanor Bumpurs in her own apartment. After a massive investigation by, again, the Beattie Commission, an HRA psychiatrist was blamed for his poor diagnosis of the woman, and the police were off the hook. Then and there, the Beattie Commission recommended total reorganization of HRA.

Watching the latest reorganization plan come together, I skeptically assumed that it would add an unnecessary layer of bureaucracy and would not solve any problems. I was very leery of this new restructuring. Trobe had been boxed in and, sadly for his staff, had chosen to leave us for the Housing Preservation Department. After replacing him as deputy commissioner for a while and coming to understand the "new" restructuring, I saw that my effectiveness was sorely diminished. And when I met my new boss, I was so unimpressed I suspected that the new plan could actually become dangerous to clients, and I began to look for a way out.

I'd been following the bizarre saga of the chief medical examiner's office in the media and thought he might need a good deputy commissioner for Administration to help him solve his problems. Dr. Elliot Gross had been fired twice by Mayor Koch after mangling some important cases, but had been reinstated by the courts on the technicality that he was a civil servant. I approached Victor Botnick, the mayor's health advisor. Botnick ran it past the mayor and received his approval. After an interview with the Health commissioner, they created the position, and it was offered to me. After seven incredible years, I left HRA.

CHAPTER 3

THE MORGUE

A S WE CLIMBED THE STAIRS to the forensics lab, an overwhelming stench assailed us. I asked Dr. Gross what it was, and he said that a half ton of organs were being stored in white tubs lining the hallway because the incinerator had broken down *and* they'd run out of refrigerated space for all the body parts that had been autopsied and tested. I asked how long the incinerator had been out of service and was told it had been inoperable for *two years*—that because of changes in emission standards, it could neither be repaired nor replaced. I asked what the plan was to solve the problem and learned there was no plan. They simply had no idea what to do. The forensic staff wore masks, but the stench was driving them crazy.

I had headed uptown to the Office of the Chief Medical Examiner (OCME), commonly known as the morgue, in the hope that I could straighten things out there. When I told some friends about my new job, they thought I was insane. "You're going to straighten out Elliot Gross's office? May God have mercy on your soul."

My appointment as a deputy commissioner of Health for administration at the morgue appeared in the New York Times on December 20, 1985. At the end of the Times article, they quoted Dr. Robert Newman, who'd taught me so much when I worked at the methadone program, and it's a quote I cherish.

Robert G. Newman, president of Beth Israel Medical Center, who was then assistant commissioner of the Health Department, praised Miss Stone's administrative abilities. "She was a very, very sharp administrator," Dr. Newman said. "She was tough when she had to be tough and flexible when she could be flexible. She had the ability to deal on a professional level with all kinds of people. That quality will stand her in good stead as the administrator in a very visible and somewhat controversial medical examiner's office."

The work of the medical examiner's office, though mostly overlooked and in the shadows, is essential to New York City. Deceased persons of unknown identity and those who die under suspicion of foul play are sent to the morgue. OCME performs about 14,000 autopsies a year, most of them on unidentified homeless or street people or victims of violent crime. The saddest autopsies are those of infants and children who are often victims of violent child abuse, many of them abandoned and forgotten, their bodies never claimed. All are buried in Potter's Field on Hart Island, the cemetery of the unknowns. In truth, very few deceased New Yorkers actually come through the morgue. If you die while under the care of a doctor either at home or in a hospital, the body usually goes straight to a funeral director for burial.

The Office of the Chief Medical Examiner was created in January 1918, when the New York State Legislature abolished the city's office of the coroner and replaced it with a chief medical examiner (CME). The coroner's office had been rife with corruption, often conspiring with the police department and other interested parties who wanted rigged autopsies of murder victims and others. In order to ensure that the CME was independent of political control, the post was given a civil service title. Under civil service rules, aspirants for the job of chief medical examiner had to take a civil service exam, and the mayor was required to appoint one of the three who scored highest.

During the modern era, from 1954 to 1974, chief medical examiner Dr. Milton Helpern established New York's OCME as the finest in the country. He was a giant in the field of forensic pathology, a medical detective one mystery writer described as "Sherlock Holmes with a microscope." His integrity and judgment were beyond reproach, and he authored books that became the standard texts for pathology and toxicology. But after Dr. Helpern's retirement in 1974, OCME began to be plagued with media reports of mixed-up bodies, severed heads, missing body parts, and allegations by the city's Department of Investigation that some of OCME's mortuary staff were receiving kickbacks from funeral directors looking for business.

Things got worse in 1978 when a young Helpern protégé, Dr. Michael Baden, was named to lead the department. Baden had an outsize ego, a natural condescension, and a reputation for grandstanding and celebrity seeking. Manhattan district attorney Robert Morgenthau and Health commissioner Reinaldo Ferrer complained to Koch that Baden had lost important evidence in homicide cases, was unresponsive to their queries and requests, and lacked both the judgment and the temperament for the job. Before his one-year probationary period was up, Mayor Koch fired him. Baden sued the city, but ultimately, the city prevailed. Years later he went on to testify in a number of high-profile murder cases, including the O.J. Simpson trial and the case of Michael Brown, whose death marked the beginning of the Black Lives Matter movement.

Enter young Dr. Elliot Gross, another Helpern protégé, who also happened to be married to Helpern's daughter. Koch appointed Elliot Gross chief medical examiner in 1979. Gross successfully passed his one-year probationary period, becoming the permanent CME in 1980. His first few years were without major problems, but in the early '80s, several prominent New York defense attorneys began accusing Gross of generating false autopsy results in police custody cases and of giving misleading testimony under oath in court.

On September 15, 1983, a 25-year-old African American man from Brooklyn, Michael Stewart, was arrested in the Union Square subway station for scrawling graffiti on the walls. While in police custody, he lapsed into a coma and died 13 days later. The six officers involved were arrested and charged with manslaughter but acquitted in a jury trial. The *New York Times* reported that Dr. Gross initially attributed Stewart's death to cardiac arrest and ruled out physical violence as a contributing factor, but several weeks later, Gross inexplicably revised his conclusion and cited a spinal cord injury as the cause of death. When questioned under oath, Gross testified that he had let stand an erroneous cause of death on his official autopsy report because of concern about how his office would be perceived. It was incredible. The Black community and much of the legal and political community were outraged, and Gross's credibility and reputation were severely damaged.

It would get worse in 1985 when the New York Times ran a series of scathing articles on Gross's leadership and performance, citing several cases in which his actions suggested medical and managerial incompetence. The articles created a firestorm. Gross subsequently sued the New York Times for libel, but the courts decided for the Times. Three separate investigations by the city, state, and federal governments followed. Two cited incompetence and mismanagement at the OCME but cleared Gross of criminal wrongdoing. During the investigations, Dr. Gross took two paid leaves of absence. When he returned, Mayor Koch was legally bound under civil service regulations to reinstate him once again.

This was the reeking, deeply troubled department I entered on a cold January morning in 1986. After I'd settled into my office, Dr. Gross came by to give me a tour of the building on First Avenue and 30th Street. He was a small, soft-spoken, and somewhat shy man in his early 50s, a dapper dresser who prided himself on his elegant neckties.

My first task was obvious. I did some research and discovered that the only viable solution for the stench on the laboratory floor was to hire a medical waste company to dispose of the organs. But because of the city's byzantine purchasing rules, authorization could take months. This was unacceptable. Then I discovered an existing "requirements" contract that the Health and Hospital Corporation (HHC) used for its medical waste removal. Since the OCME and the HHC were both city entities, I was able to arrange for us to tap into that contract. I'd found a way to avoid months of delay, and when I told Dr. Gross and the director of the forensics lab, they were pleased indeed.

The day finally came when the company arrived to remove and dispose of the half ton of organs, and the whole laboratory staff was ecstatic. I was in a meeting downtown when I got a frantic call from the lab director, who was so upset she could hardly speak. Dr. Gross had apparently stopped the waste company from touching a thing. I rushed back uptown to the building and found Dr. Gross on the fourth floor. He told me he was afraid of losing the "chain of evidence" by disposing of these thousands of rotting organs, and I reminded him that the issue had already been researched, discussed, and agreed on, that the organs were no longer evidence but decomposing waste. Then I put my hands on his shoulders, moved him slowly backward to the stairwell, and walked him back downstairs. It had taken me two weeks to remove a half ton of organs that had been rotting on the fourth floor for two years. The staff thought I was a miracle worker. They could finally breathe.

At OCME it was important for me to demonstrate that I was not intimidated by the nature of the work, so every day I made a point of walking down to the autopsy room and the basement's refrigerated rooms to take a look around. The two refrigerated rooms held about 10 bodies that were being prepared for autopsies. Other bodies, waiting for transport to either funeral directors or Hart Island, were stored in large refrigerated drawers placed all around the basement. The ambient smell was far from pleasant, but the workers put up with it, and so did I. When I talked to friends about my job, I would say everything was fine, but the truth was that for those first two weeks I could hardly eat a thing. But I got over it. When I came home in the evening and sat down to dinner, my husband said he'd give me just 10 minutes to talk about my workday. "You can have 10 minutes, no more."

During my first two weeks, I also discovered that the autopsy reports—essential for legal processing—were at least six months behind schedule and getting more and more behind every day. We hired an expert transcriber to clear the backlog. She was a blind woman who loved the work of transcribing the voice recordings doctors made at autopsies. She was fast and accurate, and with overtime for the rest of the staff, the backlog was cleared up in two months.

One day the deputy medical examiner came to my office to complain about a work stoppage. Mortuary workers had gotten into an argument and were refusing to move bodies into the autopsy rooms. The dispute was over their respective workloads and had become quite heated. I went downstairs and talked to everyone involved. I asked each person to privately tell me what their problem was and let them talk it out one by one. Then I told the four to follow me to the refrigerator drawers where the bodies were. I pulled out a drawer and said, "We're going to move this body onto the gurney." I instructed each person to grab a limb of the corpse. "Okay," I said, "one, two, three, lift!" They hoisted the body onto the gurney and wheeled it into the autopsy room. I couldn't resist telling people that I had just settled a labor dispute over someone's dead body!

I had brought my assistant, Adrienne Leaf, with me to OCME from HRA. Adrienne was a strong, smart manager, and in addition to dramas like rotting organs and backed-up autopsy reports, we of course dealt with the day-to-day items like budgets, personnel, supplies, capital purchases, and working with unions. One morning, the mortuary chief asked me to sign a paper requesting the exhumation of a body from Potter's Field. When I asked why, he told me that they'd mixed up bodies and buried someone on Hart Island whose body should have been sent to relatives in Manhattan. He couldn't explain exactly how this had happened, but apparently we'd sent those relatives an unknown and unclaimed body, which they had cremated as their own. I signed the paper and began to investigate. Adrienne assembled a team that included mortuary staff and a few police detectives who were permanently assigned to the OCME.

In a few days, we met around a large table in my office and were told how this mix-up might have occurred. We learned there were three bodies, not just two, that had been confused. It appeared that the tags had fallen off the toes of three corpses and had been reattached to the wrong toes. But who was who? And where were they? Fortunately, we'd been able to correctly identify Body C as a Native American, and his remains had already been shipped to relatives in the Southwest. His toe tag was apparently replaced correctly.

The morgue staff realized that the other two bodies had been confused, and it was determined that Body A—whose identity was unknown—had been mistakenly delivered to a family in Manhattan. Body B's toe tag had misidentified him as unknown, and he'd been transported to Hart Island and buried in Potter's Field. When the staff determined Body B's true identity, his body was exhumed and returned to the OCME . . . and it was clear that Body B's family would have to be notified of the mix-up and told that the actual remains of their relative were in the OCME morgue. There was some pushback in the room about notifying the family, with someone suggesting that we leave well enough alone and do nothing.

"Listen, there are six of us here in this room that know about this, and we can't ignore it," I said. "And I'm not going to participate in any coverup. We screwed up, and the right thing to do is to notify the family of our mistake and tell them we have their real relative in our morgue."

Adrienne Leaf phoned a sister of the deceased and left a message that we had important information about their relative and wanted to visit them and discuss it in person. When the sister finally called back a few weeks later, she said she would meet with us at her attorney's office on Madison Avenue the following week. The word *attorney* indicated that there could be big legal problems for us, not to mention unwanted media attention. I could just see the headline: "Morgue Mixes Up Bodies, Family Cremates Wrong Guy." I clearly had to visit the mayor's office to explain the situation to Victor Botnick and attorney Doron Gopstein. Telling this absurd tale about toe tags falling off and being put back wrongly, and mixing up bodies A, B, and C, was so preposterous and had such a comedic edge that after a while everybody was laughing uncontrollably. The mayor's office assigned a lawyer from the Corporation Counsel to accompany me when I met with the family.

Accompanied by the city attorney, we went to the lawyers' offices on Madison Avenue in Midtown. We sat at a conference table with two of the family's attorneys, the dead man's sister, and another relative. The deceased was a middle-aged man who had apparently been estranged from his family for some time. Most likely in an inebriated state, he died when he was hit by a subway train. He'd had plenty of identification on his person, and there was no indication of foul play. I related the story of the mix-up quietly and simply, and apologized for our mistake. The family was welcome to claim the body, and I offered to have the city pay the expense of a reburial.

"Is that all there is?" one of their attorneys asked.

"That's all there is," I said. Then they requested a few minutes to discuss it. Fifteen minutes later, one of their lawyers returned and told us they'd be in touch.

We didn't hear from the family or their attorneys for some time, so finally we called and asked if the sister would please come in and at least identify her relative. Reluctantly, she agreed. In the morgue, she took one quick glance at the corpse and said, "That's not him." She did not claim the body, so back he went to Potter's Field. We could never figure out why the family reacted the way they did. We knew the body we had was their relative; what could have been their relationship to him? It was and still is a mystery. Because of this episode, I decided that toe tags were too problematic, and from then on, each body was identified by an ankle bracelet not unlike the wrist bracelets used in hospitals.

I arrived one morning to find the entire building occupied by dozens of Hasidic Jewish men in full regalia—black hats, black suits, white shirts. From an ultra-strict Orthodox sect, one of their own was in the morgue, and they were clamoring to claim the body a.s.a.p. By Jewish law, they had to bury their dead within 24 hours—no time for bureaucracy. And they had incredible political clout. I had at least 100 calls on my phone from every politician in the tri-state area asking about the release of this body. We expedited the process pronto, and off they went with their deceased.

Except for a few highly charged incidents, Dr. Gross was almost always friendly and cooperative. He was quite the gentleman, and every morning he and his driver would pick me up outside my apartment building in his official city vehicle and take me to work.

A few times a year, something big happened at the OCME, something that would be widely reported in the media. In April 1986, Donald Manes, the 52-year-old Queens borough president and political heavyweight, committed suicide in his home in Queens. That night my phone rang at 11:30 p.m. I was asleep, and my husband answered. Elliot Gross was on the line: "You better wake Bonnie; this is a big one. We don't want to lose this body." Manes's body had been brought to the Queens morgue, and Dr. Gross had ordered it transferred to the main office in Manhattan, which had better facilities and security.

A jovial, outspoken character, Donald Manes had been an extremely popular Democratic Queens borough president from 1971 to 1986. In the past year, however, he was rumored to have been involved in a Parking Violations Bureau scandal. The Department of Transportation (DOT) had signed a huge contract to develop a cutting-edge, handheld device for issuing and recording parking tickets. At the direction of Manes, Geoffrey Lindenauer, a senior staff member at the DOT, had made certain that a company called Citisource would secure this valuable contract. The deal was that Lindenauer and Manes would each receive significant stock in Citisource if the company was awarded the contract. Yet another political boss, Stanley Friedman, was also implicated in the scheme as a player for Citisource.

As the investigation dragged on, Manes had already made one suicide attempt by cutting the veins in his legs. A few months later he tried again and succeeded. With Manes's body in the morgue, the next day was a nightmare. The police surrounded the OCME. Dozens of print and TV reporters showed up for details about the suicide and the autopsy, but Dr. Gross was bivouacked in his office and refused to come out. Another forensic pathologist had performed the autopsy, but Gross refused to talk to the press or, for that matter, to anybody.

Around 3 p.m., I got a call from City Hall. Dr. Gross had phoned them to complain that I was harassing him. I said, "Are you kidding? The whole world wants his comments, and he won't come out of his office." All the press wanted was some sort of comment or statement from Gross, really anything. They were frantic for any morsel of information. Gross could simply have said that the autopsy was still under review and the cause of death was still unclear, even though the truth was that a kitchen knife was stuck in Donald Manes's chest. But Gross wouldn't respond at all. He'd always been traumatized by the press and, when I left for the day, was still locked in his office. Days passed, and finally the press stopped calling. The only statement from the OCME would be that the cause of death remained "pending chemical analysis."

Several days later, I discussed the case with Dr. Gross. He explained a grim detail to me. Because of heavy bone and muscle in the chest, it is almost impossible to stab oneself in the heart. Gross said that without a doubt, Manes had placed the knife against a wall, leaned on the blade, and pushed himself into it using his body weight to force the knife in.

In my black humor moments, I'd say that I was responsible for the death of Donald Manes. Eight years earlier, when I was in charge of operations for the Addiction Services Agency, there was a staff member named Geoffrey Lindenauer whom Commissioner Bernie Bihari and I had found unfit for his job because he refused to manage and discipline the drug treatment service contractors in Queens. We knew Lindenauer was politically "protected" by Manes, but we fired him anyway. We waited for the other political shoe to drop, but nothing happened. There was only silence. Then we learned that Lindenauer had been given a job at the Department of Transportation. Eight years after that, the parking meter scandal broke open, and Geoffrey and his good buddy and protector, Donald Manes, were facing major charges. Lindenauer had been the bagman and had turned state's evidence before Manes committed suicide. I figured I was responsible, because if we hadn't fired Lindenauer, he wouldn't have had that corrupt opportunity at DOT, and Manes would still be alive.

One day the mortuary supervisor came to my office and told me we had to hire a refrigerated truck. When I asked why, he said, "Well, they took the boat out of service." Boat . . . what boat? I had no idea what he was talking about. He explained that he had gotten a call from the Department of Transportation saying the ferryboat that came to the morgue once a week to transport bodies for burial on Hart Island was scheduled for a complete renovation and would no longer be able to make the trip. I asked how long the repairs would take, and he said they'd told him it would be about 18 months.

"You must be kidding," I said. "Let me get this straight: if we are going to be without a ferry for a year and a half, what are we going to do with the bodies?"

"That's why I need the refrigerated trucks," he answered. "We'll store them in the trucks." I immediately called the Department of Transportation and got a bit of a runaround. Then I called the new DOT commissioner, Ross Sandler, whom I knew only slightly. His response was totally unsatisfactory: "We have to do this ferry renovation, you know, because we have capital money designated for the project and the work is already scheduled."

I took a deep breath and said, "Okay, Ross, since we have no space to store 18 months of corpses, we will rent and park refrigerated trucks stacked with bodies while we wait for your ferry to be renovated and back in service."

Ross stammered a bit and said, "Well, what do you want me to do?"

I replied that I was sure he could find a way to substitute that ferryboat with another one for just 18 months.

"I don't know if I can," he said.

"Okay then, do you want me to call the mayor and let him know we'll be parking trucks loaded with dead bodies all the way down First Avenue? They're likely to reach City Hall in very short order."

"Very funny," he said.

And I said, "Well, if you prefer, you can call the mayor yourself and explain it." He found us another ferry.

Ferryboats seemed to be deliberately working their way into my life. It started when I worked for the Coast Guard on Governor's Island and had to take the ferry back and forth every single day, getting seasick on almost every 10-minute ride. Later, I was made captain of the retired *Gold Star Mother* during its service as a methadone clinic, and then, years later, when I was at HRA, a strange item showed up in our budget: a ferryboat. Somehow, charges for the ferry conveying bodies from the morgue to Hart Island were being inexplicably charged to us.

Every year OCME had a fundraising gala to support the Milton Helpern Forensic Library and Museum, which was housed on the top floor of the morgue. The library was a strange place indeed, with murder weapons of all kinds as well as other assorted macabre memorabilia. My husband and I were invited. I couldn't imagine who would be interested in attending such a gala, but it was mobbed with four of the city's district attorneys and their staffs, forensic pathologists from all over the region, and laboratory toxicology experts. A group of mystery writers took two tables. My husband began to refer to it as the Coroner's Ball. He sat next to OCME's chief toxicologist, a young, dark-haired woman with a deep foreign accent.

"Where are you from?" he asked her.

"I am from Transylvania."

When I announced that I was leaving the medical examiner's office, Mayor Koch appointed a Medical Advisory Board headed by Dr. Martin Cherkasky, a preeminent physician and healthcare expert. Dr. Cherkasky and I met so that I could relate some of my experiences and insights. About a year later, the medical board recommended that Dr. Gross be removed from the job due to his poor management, leaving out any judgment of his medical competence. Dr. Cherkasky later told me that had I stayed at OCME, they could not have removed Gross based on managerial issues, since I had made so many improvements. Dr. Gross went on to serve as chief medical examiner in Lake County, Indiana, and later in Cape May, New Jersey.

The city put together a three-person professional panel to recommend a new chief medical examiner to the mayor. Their choice was Dr. Charles Hirsch, who had been medical examiner for Suffolk County. Mayor Koch appointed him in 1989, and Hirsch successfully led the office for almost 25 years, reviving its once-sterling reputation.

In 2001, 15 years after I left, the Office of the Chief Medical Examiner played a major role in the aftermath of the September 11 terror attacks. Bodies and body parts were sent to the OCME for identification, and doctors and the laboratory staff pledged to work until everyone was identified. After 16 years of painstaking work, only 1,113 of the 2,753 people who died at the World Trade Center were positively identified. The unidentified remains are interred underground in a temperature-controlled vault beneath the memorial site.

CHAPTER 4

WORKING ON THE RAILROAD

A FEW MONTHS INTO MY JOB at the medical examiner's office, I got a call from Bruce McIver, the new president of the Long Island Railroad, whom I knew from his work as the director of the city's Office of Labor Relations. We made plans to have lunch, and I assumed he was trying to help someone get a job at the medical examiner's office, but to my amazement, McIver offered me a job working on the railroad. He felt that my extensive government experience was a solid foundation for managing the public side of the railroad: public information, political relations, press relations, and marketing.

All I knew about trains was that I loved them (the subway too), but other than occasionally riding the LIRR to Long Island, I knew next to nothing about them. When I told McIver that, he suggested I have a talk with a few railroad insiders, which I did. I also spoke with my brother Lewis (my constant advisor), and of course spent quite a bit of time mulling over the idea. There was no doubt in my mind that the railroad would provide plenty of action and a whole new set of challenges. I accepted the offer but told McIver that I would have to remain at the ME's office for a while longer, but that if he could wait for a few more months, I'd take the job. We had a deal.

When I started work at the LIRR in 1986, it needed a serious overhaul. Founded in 1824, the Long Island Railroad was the nation's biggest, busiest commuter railroad, even though it never turned a profit. By the 1950s, it was subsidized by the state. In 1965 the state bought and absorbed the Long Island Railroad into the Metropolitan Transportation Authority. Each year, the LIRR transported 89.3 million passengers, 354,800 people on the average weekday, when 75 percent of Long Islanders commuted back and forth to work in the city. The railroad is a crucial part of Long Island life and of the financial health of the city and state. Trains run 24 hours a day on 700 miles of track; there are 11 different lines and 124 stations. It had been a commercial railroad, but by the time the MTA took over, it was bankrupt. The railroad was essential to the region, and rather than shut it down, the state purchased it. Long Islanders were heavily dependent on the trains, and unless you worked very odd hours in very odd places, you rode the rails.

Still, the railroad was a man's world where grown-up boys played with trains. On day one of my initiation tour, I met the men who handled the control room, the railroad's command center. Several engineers and analysts who handled operations invited me into the control room, where they monitored huge screens mapping out the various lines and how they performed. The operations people told me that most fatal accidents at the 300 railroad crossings were suicides or automobiles that got stuck on the tracks. They described in gruesome detail accident scenes certain to unnerve the new "girl." Of course, they had no idea that I'd just spent six months managing the city morgue. I started asking all kinds of detailed questions about the fatalities— what kinds of injuries, profiles of those killed, plus the railroad's relationship with the police and medical examiners in Nassau and Suffolk Counties. Word got around that the new "girl" on staff was not exactly naïve, and they didn't quite know what to make of me.

As soon as I arrived, a strike was looming, which immediately drew everyone into the labor negotiations with the railroad's 14 unions. McIver was a well-known labor negotiator, having spearheaded New York City's Office of Labor Relations and, later, the Metropolitan Transportation Authority. He was a powerful and imposing presence who hardly ever smiled. McIver was from Montana, and New Yorkers thought he was the mythic "Marlboro Man." Mayor Koch even called him Cool Hand Luke and said, "He has ice water running through his veins."

Months before the strike, McIver had made significant progress negotiating with most of the unions, including the largest and most powerful union, the trainmen. Long Island railroad unions were the oldest in the country and extremely powerful. Politicians from both parties were on their side, and the unions deployed plenty of bravado at the negotiating table. McIver had already settled with about 40 percent of the 14 unions, each of which negotiated separately. But although they negotiated separately, they worked in solidarity, so when the Engineers' Union, a small but very important one, balked, a strike was on. Joe Cassidy, the well-respected, usually laid-back head of that union, had been royally goaded by a few colleagues, and with great macho flourish, Cassidy called a strike.

A strike on the LIRR devastates the entire New York City region. Plans for alternative transportation were made, but in reality, there was and is no substitute for the train. In 1987, 150,000 regular commuters were stranded as 354,000 trips a day, including all off-peak rides, were canceled. The nightmare went on for two weeks, and to make matters worse, there were two large snowstorms during the strike, making travel by car agonizing if not impossible. Effectively managing our relationship with political leaders and the media was key to how the railroad would be publicly perceived, and even before the strike was called, my public affairs staff created a guide that itemized all the railroad's basic facts: budget figures, the number of employees in each of the 14 unions, the names of the union leaders, a history of former strikes, the number of trains, the number of passengers, details on labor laws, and bargaining issues at play in the looming strike. The issues and the players were quite complicated, and the guide became indispensable, especially for a press that knew very little about running a railroad.

The press was with us in hotels in Manhattan and at JFK airport in Queens during round-the-clock negotiations. The only way for us to maintain credibility was to keep ourselves available for questions and to make sure everyone had a copy of the guide. Most importantly, we decided to focus on an issue a day for the press and to provide all backup facts and information so that they could write a daily story. In 1987 there was constant radio news; there were daily papers and nightly television. The various press outlets had different filing deadlines, and each reporter needed to have something to report to meet their deadline every single day. Because we supplied them with interesting stories, they stuck close, and we were able to keep media control even as political and public anger escalated.

The MTA assumed we wouldn't know what we were doing, since we were just the railroad and not the Metropolitan Transportation Authority. Their press office was ready to step in but never did because the media had everything they needed from us. The MTA was surprised, and it was a huge feather in our cap. I'm not at all sure that the same strategy would work in today's speed-of-light news cycle, but it worked then.

Political pressure to end the strike was overwhelming and came from all sides—from local officeholders to the governor and senators. More than once I heard Governor Mario Cuomo and Senator Alfonse D'Amato screaming over the phone at Bruce McIver to end the damn strike. At the very least, we'd succeeded in keeping the media focused on the issues instead of just savaging us.

When it appeared that the strike was about to end, senior management met to discuss the restoration of train service. After some back-and-forth, McIver asked Lawrence Baggerly, the vice president of Operations, how long it would take to reinstate service. Baggerly thought for a few minutes and said, "Four days." I leaped to my feet and yelled, "No way! Are you crazy? Four more days after a 13-day strike?" Everyone in the room got upset. Railroad police chief Joe Flynn stood up, ready to stop a fight. From my perspective, anything longer than "the next day" would create havoc with the public and the press. McIver instructed me to calm down, and eventually, two days was agreed upon.

Then we started building a case for the public as to why we needed that much time: after two major snowstorms and with more than 700 miles of tracks, every rail, switch, signal light, station platform, station stairway, grade crossing, bridge, and tunnel had to be plowed, de-iced, tested, and approved for safety. And trains needed to be repositioned before they could safely roll. I published a comprehensive list of all the work that had to be done to get the trains back in service, which helped us avoid criticism during the two-day delay. But the two-week strike was over. The final settlement did not achieve any gains beyond the existing deals McIver had originally negotiated. It achieved nothing new for workers, who had pointlessly lost two weeks of pay. It should never have happened.

After the strike, my job at the railroad was far less dramatic but no less challenging. The LIRR was a favorite scapegoat, and commuters delighted in excoriating train service. Many were professionals with time on their hands to analyze operations ad nauseam as they rode back and forth to work every day. (This was long before cell phones and laptops kept them on the job even in transit.) They meticulously clocked every flaw: late trains, surly conductors, dirty cars, overcrowding. Train cars actually *were* filthy—strewn with discarded newspapers, coffee cups, soda cans, and all manner of things riders leave behind. Every attempted anti-litter campaign failed miserably, so most LIRR senior staff assumed that any new initiative would fail too . . . but they humored us. And because cleaning up was a natural job for a "girl," they were all in.

But the "boys" didn't know who they were dealing with. They assumed I'd put up cute posters to scold people and urge them to stop littering, but I knew it would take more than posters to keep the trains clean. My background was in operations and I saw things through that lens, so the first thing we did was to study the problem. We realized that a coordinated and sustained effort was necessary. I put together a task force that included personnel from several departments, and we worked together to create a plan. It was critical that every LIRR department buy into the plan wholeheartedly . . . and they did.

To establish a benchmark, we started by weighing trash coming off the trains every night, as well as trash in bins on the platforms. Then we talked through the best placement for the trash receptacles. For safety's sake, we decided not to put them in the cars, but train platforms would need many, many more. We had the Stations Department work out a system for managing increased trash throughout the day. We developed a customer communications strategy that included seat notices, posters in the trains, stickers on the backs of seats visible to passengers, and finally and most importantly, an agreement that conductors would add anti-littering requests to their regular station announcements. We developed new signage, ordered new trash cans, created new work schedules for maintenance staff, and finally, wrote the script for conductors: *Please take your coffee cups and newspapers with you when you exit the train.*

The new anti-littering campaign began in a carefully coordinated fashion, but even in the first few days it clearly wasn't working. The amount of litter stayed the same. Then I sent my entire staff out to ride the trains and monitor them. After several days, they reported that the conductors were not making consistent announcements. After sharing staff findings with the task force, we pressed the Operations Department to step up enforcement of conductor announcements.

A little background here: conductors (overwhelmingly male) have always been sensitive about being viewed as "airline stewardesses" instead of professional railroad people, so they'd balked at our instructions. But we insisted their managers take it seriously, and finally, they came down on conductors who'd refused to incorporate the anti-litter request in announcements. And, after some mighty huffing and puffing, they got the message.

Commuters got the message too, and began picking up after themselves, carting their newspapers, coffee containers, and other litter to the now-plentiful waste bins on the platforms. Trains grew measurably cleaner. We weighed the trash from the cars and compared it to the weight recorded before the campaign began. There was a huge difference—from 9½ pounds of litter per car to 3½. Several weeks later, an opinion study confirmed that passengers were seeing significantly less litter than before. Our anti-litter campaign had exceeded expectations, even the conductors agreed. Newspapers, including the *New York Times* and *Newsday*, picked up the story of the Long Island Railroad's successful anti-litter campaign that triumphed because everyone—riders, conductors, and station staff—pitched in to do their part.

Metro-North, our "sister" commuter railroad in Westchester, followed suit and also attempted to reduce littering. But they didn't inquire after our methods, and their program had virtually no beneficial effect. The *New York Times* reported that LIRR's anti-littering effort was more successful than Metro-North's. Metro-North blamed the passengers, but I blamed management.

I noticed that the main LIRR station in Jamaica, Queens, had no identifying signage . . . not at the entrances, at the exits, on the platforms, anywhere. When I queried my colleagues, the response was, *Well, everybody knows it's Jamaica.* They saw no need for signs, but I persisted, and eventually, the signs went up. I saw, too, that there were confusing signs everywhere reading "eastbound" and "westbound." Since the whole railroad line was east of the city, NYC was actually west, so the signs made no sense. I suggested new, clear signage for every station: "Direction to New York City" and "Direction to Points East." I anticipated a fight, but the idea was so simple and obvious, everyone readily agreed. In record time, all stations had accurate signage. Even today, when I ride the LIRR, I feel proud when I see it. Often, the simplest and most easily overlooked solutions are the best.

In January 1988, the MTA decided to ban smoking on trains. Riders who smoked regarded this as quite an assault on their freedom, but by utilizing the same systematic approach we'd used with our anti-littering campaign, gradually we got them to accept and adhere to the no-smoking policy. Once again, Metro-North tried the same, but there was open rebellion. Metro-North blamed their "spoiled" commuters, and once again, I blamed management.

When homeless people sleeping and living in Grand Central Station, Metro-North's terminal, became a major issue, my experience with the homeless and the press stood me in good stead. The homeless and some of their very vocal advocates had literally taken over Grand Central, using it to demonstrate their plight of being pushed around and mistreated by insensitive Metro-North police. Advocates distributed food, held candlelight vigils, and used the behavior of Metro-North's police to curry sympathy. The LIRR's Penn Station was also a safe, warm place to sleep, but I was determined to keep the homeless who slept there very low key and out of the limelight. Working with our police chief, Joe Flynn, we stayed under the press's radar. We also worked closely with the city's shelter staff to offer shelter to all the men and women sleeping in Penn Station and instructed our police to be polite and try to work out arrangements with the homeless as to where and when they could sleep in peace yet stay out of the way of commuters. As a result, all the negative publicity and protests occurred at Grand Central Station, not Penn.

Naturally oblivious to many things, I finally noticed that for staff, simply going to the ladies' room in LIRR headquarters in Jamaica was a ridiculous ordeal, since the ladies' room on the executive floor had only one toilet, whereas the men's room had three! We women would stand single file in a narrow hallway waiting our turn. I usually didn't notice inconveniences, but this began to annoy me. When I brought it up at our weekly vice presidents' meeting, everyone immediately agreed it was a problem. However, the VP of Operations said that renovating the ladies' room would have to wait for the second five-year capital plan—at least three years away!

I made it quite clear to the group that this really wouldn't do and brought it up a few more times before realizing that again, they were just humoring me. The railroad was a man's world. There was not a whiff of women's liberation anywhere, and sure enough, in no time, my fellow vice presidents started grumbling about me. At one meeting I was actually told there were "no women" on the executive floor and that they had conducted a study to prove it—but their study didn't include the secretaries and clerical staff.

I quietly went around to all the secretaries and asked each one what she thought of the bathroom situation. They hated it. Then I asked if they'd join me in taking over the men's room, an idea they relished! I asked them to *please keep the takeover a secret.* They agreed, but I knew it would get out anyway, and that all the male vice presidents would be furious, which was exactly what I wanted. I heard through the grapevine that one VP said, "She better be prepared to stare down some dick if she does that." Bruce McIver's young executive assistant responded, "I don't know. . . . If I were you, I'd be prepared to have your dicks stared at."

One day I went to see Ben Dwinnell, the railroad's construction director, who reported to a vice president not generally included in the weekly meetings. I closed the door of Dwinnell's office and brought up the ladies' room controversy. He knew all about it, of course, but I said, "You know, Ben, I don't like surprises, so I wanted to tell you personally that if something is not done about this in 30 days, we're going to change the sign on the door of the men's room to say, 'The Ben Dwinnell Ladies' Room.' Just wanted to let you know."

"Ha ha," he said, "very funny." But it did the trick, because in the next three weeks they reconstructed the space, adding two more toilets and sinks. When it was completed, the VP of Operations presented me with a pink hard hat. The women on the floor were ecstatic. They started saying, *I hope Bonnie gets pregnant, because then maybe we can get some child care here.*

I had never before experienced sexism in the workplace, but at the railroad it was so ubiquitous it was almost comical. Secretaries were referred to as "the girls," and in 1986, the blatant lack of better employment opportunities and advancement for women was the sad reality. In 2007 the MTA appointed Helena Williams the first woman president of the Long Island Railroad. She served in that post for seven years, until 2014—a record for longevity.

I became quite close to Sybil Williams, the newly hired director of Human Resources. Sybil was an older African American woman with considerable experience in the corporate world, and she once told me she thought many LIRR employees went home at night and donned white hoods.

"Come on, Sybil, don't exaggerate. This is Long Island, not Mississippi. And it's 1987, not 1950."

But in her inimitable, wise voice, Sybil responded, "I'm telling you the truth." Charges of discrimination in all MTA divisions, including Metro-North, buses, subways, and the Bridge and Tunnel Authority, prompted the MTA to commission a professional attitude survey of management staff in all their divisions. At first the consultants thought something had gone terribly wrong with the data. They redid the survey, and this time, they even did it by hand. But the outcome was the same. The results described a company management with attitudes resembling those in the state of Alabama in the 1950s. The consultants had never seen anything like it. The railroad was a closed society. Among many other things, it was a well-known fact that someone could only be an authentic "railroad man" if his grandfather and father had each spent 30 years working for the railroad. Just having a father who worked on the railroad didn't qualify. The old-timers were mostly of English and German ancestry, with a smattering of Irish. Managers were so in the dark ages that their concept of integration was "allowing" Italians to be gang foremen on the tracks.

Whenever thorny problems arose, management assigned them to me. For sure they loved their trains, but anything to do with passengers, politics, or communities was of no interest to them at all. They referred to some of us who'd been hired by McIver as carpetbaggers: "All Bonnie knows is Penn Station, the Hamptons, and a whole lot of little towns with Indian names in between," said Ed Yule, the head of the trainmen's union.

In its first five-year capital plan, the issue of parking spaces around the stations became important, since for the first time in decades there was money for expansion. The problem was how to allocate dollars—how to decide which towns and villages would get more parking, since some stations were obviously overcrowded. This was going to become a political hot potato in many communities on the Island, so the boys were more than happy to hand the issue over to me. I realized that a thorough study had to be done to back up whatever decisions we'd recommend; anything less would lead us into a political quagmire. I enlisted the help of Dan Caufield, the director of Capital Planning. Dan rented a helicopter and flew around taking aerial photos of all the stations and their parking lots. Fortunately, the answers were obvious even to the naked eye, and we subsequently plotted new parking allocations. We compiled a very slick report and included all the aerial photos.

I knew the MTA Board would inevitably bring up the issue of passenger capacity on trains at those stations with an enhanced number of parking spaces and, consequently, a greater number of commuters, so before we went to the board with our final recommendations, I had my staff do a study of passenger counts. For decades, the railroad did passenger counts twice a year as a basis for planning routes and schedules. My staff found the passenger-count documentation related to each station slated for new parking to determine whether there would be room on the trains for additional passengers. I was quite skeptical about whether this would help us, but I knew we had to have all the facts in hand. But when my staff presented me with the results, I questioned them. They made no sense in view of the well-known experience of severe overcrowding during rush hours. I sent everybody back to the drawing board, but they returned with the same data.

Then I looked at the records myself. Sure enough, there were 30,000 empty seats on rush hour trains going into Penn Station each morning! The reality was there were only about 20 trains out of more than 100, total, that were overcrowded, with standing room only. The common wisdom about rush hour overcrowding was simply not borne out by the facts, and I discovered that the long-standing myth about overcrowding at Jamaica Station, the railroad's hub, was totally wrong.

Operations staff was convinced that overcrowding was so bad that only a huge renovation of the entire station and its tracks could remedy it. The image of painfully crowded trains rumbling through Jamaica Station every morning at rush hour had informed their perception, and no one questioned it. Five hundred million dollars had been set aside in the capital plan just for Jamaica Station, and work on the new elevators was already under way. But by studying the data that the railroad had collected every six months for decades, we learned that in reality, 80 of the 100 trains had plenty of seats to spare. On this railroad, individual trains had a maximum of 12 cars. The 20 overcrowded trains were so perfectly timed that commuters refused to adjust their schedules either 10 minutes earlier or later in order to get a seat. I planned how to break the news.

First, I called in Jim Yaeger, who was responsible for the entire rolling fleet. When I presented him with our findings, he had the same reaction I'd had—*It can't be true.* "You must have misplaced a decimal point. Bonnie, it's probably 3,000 seats, not 30,000." I asked him to look the data over carefully, and he, too, was stunned by what we had uncovered in the railroad's own documentation. No doubt there were overcrowded trains passing through Jamaica Station in the mornings, but only 20 out of 100 trains were "standing room only."

I started strategizing how we would present this to McIver, to the MTA Board, and to the public. Almost half a billion dollars, nearly half of the LIRR five-year capital plan, had been allocated for the expansion and reconstruction of Jamaica Station in order to alleviate perceived overcrowding. Plans had been made to add flyover tracks and widen the whole corridor. When we finally discussed it with McIver, he saw the problem immediately. Now we had to figure out how to explain to the public that a major premise of our capital plan was based on a miscalculation, and the plan would have to be revised. The system had been so starved for capital for so long, it would be easy to find other projects to fund with that "flyover" money.

It was not my role to rewrite the capital plan, but I was concerned about managing public perception. Far, far different from the world of social and human services, hard, cold facts made this problem solving easier. After all, a lot of money had already been spent drawing up plans, and the actual physical work on the elevators and escalators at Jamaica Station was well under way. In the end, there was remarkably little public fallout, because cold facts told the story. Construction already completed at Jamaica would increase handicapped accessibility, a formidable public issue. But the rest of the Jamaica rebuilding plan was scrapped, and the money was redirected to buying new, much-needed train cars. Working on the railroad, I observed that bureaucracies hardly ever question their myths. It took new eyes looking at volumes of old data to uncover the truth.

And there was yet another myth: that LIRR ridership numbers had been flat for many years. There was some interest on the part of the MTA Board in encouraging additional commuters to take the train rather than drive, but a full-blown marketing campaign had to be mounted to convince Long Islanders to take the train and leave their cars at home. Not being a marketing expert, I realized I needed professional expertise before I could present a plan, so I hired Deloitte Touche consultants to do some research before proceeding. Once again, their research exploded the common wisdom about ridership. Once again, by using the railroad's own data, the consultants mapped out that overall ridership as measured by ticket sales was indeed flat, but that that specific data actually masked two significant and opposing trends. Rush hour ridership was declining slightly, but off-peak ridership was increasing. The commuters were already there—75 percent of people who had full-time jobs in NYC rode the train. This finding was a surprise to everyone.

We developed a resonant marketing plan to promote all kinds of off-peak ridership over and above the daily commuting, which was already saturated. Fast-forward from 1986 to 2016: the commuter portion of the LIRR service dropped by 5 percent, but off-peak ridership increased a whopping 64 percent, as our 1988 marketing study had predicted. The notion of an ever-increasing, overwhelming commuter market was put to rest.

The railroad underwent many capital improvements during McIver's tenure. Eighteen miles of new electric service replaced diesel trains on one route, a brand-new rail yard on the west side of Manhattan beyond Penn Station was constructed, and a state-of-the-art repair shop was built in Hillside, Queens. New double-decker trains were purchased. New signage was installed, and air-conditioning on trains was improved. Portions of Penn Station were rebuilt, and not just litter but smoking and the sale of alcoholic beverages on the trains disappeared.

I had one major regret during my time at the LIRR. In 1988 the Barnum & Bailey Circus offered me a ride into the city on one of their elephants that every year famously traversed the Midtown Tunnel from Queens to Manhattan for the circus's annual Madison Square Garden performance. I could kick myself for declining the offer, having decided that a 2 a.m. trip was impossible for me, since I usually dropped into bed exhausted at 10. I'd never fully appreciated the "showbiz" part of government service and viewed this stunt as frivolous. But I passed up a completely unique experience. I was so obsessed with getting the job done, I couldn't enjoy the fun.

After five productive but rugged years and despite significant accomplishments, Bruce McIver left the railroad in late 1989 after disagreements with the chairman of the MTA. Since I was clearly a part of those McIver years, I was rather frozen out by the new acting president, Peter Stangl. I wasn't actually fired, but it became obvious that I wouldn't be part of the new team. Working on the railroad was loaded with action and full of challenges, but although I'd be sorry to leave, I began looking for another job.

CHAPTER 5

SELFHELP COMMUNITY SERVICES

"In my country, we took care of our people."

NOW I STARTED LOOKING for executive-level work. I began networking, and after receiving a few offers that didn't really interest me, I answered a blind ad in the *New York Times*. I soon got a call from the human-resources director of Selfhelp Community Services, a distinguished not-for-profit. I interviewed with the HR director, and Selfhelp's executive director, Richard Aronson, joined us. Aronson remembered me from my work on the Home Attendant Program in HRA years before. He was thrilled that I was interested in joining them and immediately offered me the position of chief deputy executive director.

Selfhelp Community Services was founded in 1936 by German émigrés who originally met in the apartment of a New School professor. The organization's first goal and sole purpose was to help victims of the Holocaust who'd been able to escape and immigrate to New York. Originally, Selfhelp social workers met Jewish refugees at the docks and helped them find work and places to live. As the years went by, Selfhelp social workers scoured the city's grocery stores, butcher shops, synagogues, and bus and train stations, searching for survivors who might be in need of medical or financial help, home care, or perhaps just a sympathetic ear. Selfhelp's most famous founding member was the American-German philosopher and Lutheran theologian Paul Tillich, who coined Selfhelp's motto:

We listen sensitively and we react spontaneously. Tillich served on Self-help's board of directors for 15 years.

Often refugees were trained and hired as home-care workers to help in the homes of wealthier New Yorkers. Many of these émigrés had had professional careers in Europe as doctors, teachers, or other professionals, but in America, they wound up working basic service jobs. As the refugee community expanded during and after World War II, Selfhelp became well known to many, and in the late '60s, when New York City government expanded home-care programs for the elderly and the disabled, Selfhelp was poised to become a major player in the field. Selfhelp opened senior citizen centers and developed subsidized housing programs for the elderly.

By the time I joined Selfhelp in 1990, in addition to acting as a major support for remaining Holocaust survivors, the organization had created more than 1,000 units of housing, managed six senior citizen centers, and employed 2,000 hourly home-care workers. I came to Selfhelp Community Services with substantial experience dealing with many of those issues, so my new position was a perfect fit, yet in comparison to working in government, where the phone never stopped ringing, Selfhelp seemed sleepy. Indeed, I sometimes felt like I'd been put out to pasture. No one hounded me or gave me any mountains to climb. The job *was* worthy and important, but I missed the action and had trouble winding down to a slower pace. Paul Dickstein, a former city budget director, said he'd had the same shock when he left government: *Yeah, now you're just a "guy" sitting in an office. Nobody calls, and if you want to accomplish anything, you have to reach out and stir things up.*

Still, at Selfhelp I worked with many talented and uniquely devoted people. I learned a great deal about the financial challenges and the particular difficulties of running a not-for-profit. But above all, at Selfhelp I learned the tremendous importance of a not-for-profit's board of directors. It was a revelation to me.

Aside from the citywide services for the elderly, Selfhelp's primary mission was to serve elderly Holocaust survivors. In 1990, Holocaust survivors were very elderly, all of them having been born well before 1945. They were young during the Holocaust, and most of their relatives were murdered by the Nazis. Now, 45 years later, having taken care of themselves in New York for decades, many found themselves isolated and in poor health. Those without families or financial means called Selfhelp their "last remaining relative." Caseworkers made sure these survivors received all the financial assistance they were entitled to—from both the German government and that of the United States.

Elly Kover, director of Nazi Victim Services, managed a special group of social workers who devoted their time to ensuring that the last years of survivors' lives were not only stable and secure, but also filled with well-deserved joy. Elly's unit created a monthly "Coffee Shop" program, including much-loved classical music, to try to re-create the social life survivors had enjoyed decades before in Europe. Today, more than 76 years after the end of World War II, Selfhelp continues to play a vital role in the lives of thousands.

I came to know the second generation of Selfhelp board members, who were following in their parents' footsteps supporting survivors of Nazi persecution. Selfhelp's Jewish board members were quite different from the larger Jewish community in NYC. The New York Jewish culture that I knew was generally far more aggressive, brazen, and loud (think the voluble and flamboyant late mayor, Ed Koch), but Selfhelp's board members were highly educated and refined, and devoted to the fine arts, especially classical music. Mostly successful businessmen, they were conservatively well dressed, unfailingly polite, and elegant. They also were not particularly religious. The two groups barely knew the other existed.

I became especially close to two board members. One, I'll call by his initials, PK, because I know that even though he's passed, he'd want to remain anonymous. As a young man in Germany, PK frustrated his family, who found him brash and crude, so he left to join the French Foreign Legion. Eventually, he made his way to the United States, where he became a prosperous businessman. PK was financially generous toward Selfhelp and other organizations, as well as with his extended family. I once took him to visit a shelter for homeless families, where he was deeply shocked to see such helpless poverty. He said, "Just a few wealthy people could solve this housing

problem in New York. In my country, we took care of our people."
Remembering his family's Holocaust experience, I was surprised
to hear him say this, but he regarded the Holocaust as an isolated
horror, not a way of life. PK made extraordinarily large donations,
always anonymously.

Hans Schindler was a chemist (once, when we were walking
through the snow together, I mentioned something about the salt
on the street, and Hans went into a full chemical analysis of the salt
used expressly for that purpose), a gentle soul who seemed to understand everything. (He was not the Schindler of *Schindler's List*.) He
was extremely well read, fluent in five languages, and a patron of the
arts who was also a recognized expert in brewing espresso! He told
me he had left Germany as a very young man with the full support of
his family, who had perceived the danger ahead. My husband, who
was working in City Hall at the time, arranged for him to be appointed to the Mayoral Immigration Task Force, an appointment for
which Schindler felt extremely honored and proud. We'd been good
friends for a few years when I suggested that he might need a cane,
since his walking was shaky. Hans was so furious with me, he went
out and got a personal trainer to help him strengthen his legs. A cane
was out of the question! Hans Schindler was a dear friend to me, a
treasure of a man who lived to be 92.

Selfhelp board members took their responsibilities very seriously. Once a year without fail they held a gala, a major money-raising
event. The gala was always a concert at Lincoln Center. Unlike at
any other organization's gala events, there were no introductions, no
speeches. Nobody introduced anyone from Selfhelp or presented
any of the musicians. The conductor led the orchestra, and the audience applauded in a manner so politely subdued I couldn't tell if they
enjoyed themselves or not.

At Selfhelp I was able to expand home-care services even further,
and we applied for and received a rare state license to establish a Certified Home Health Care agency, which enabled us to hire nurses
and to supervise medical care for our clients.

Homelessness remained a critical issue, and after 1992, when the
city invited nonprofits to enter the fray, it was natural that Selfhelp

venture into the homeless services arena. I saw an opportunity to open a shelter at the Holland Hotel on West 42nd Street and convinced the board to apply to manage it as a shelter for elderly, single men and women. At the same time, we'd undertaken merger negotiations with another large nonprofit agency, inevitably triggering a review of the Selfhelp board. The board was worried that our involvement with the Holland Hotel and homeless services would jeopardize the merger deal, so we withdrew our application to manage the hotel. The merger negotiations fell apart too, so no merger and no Holland Hotel. I learned the valuable lesson that nonprofits and their boards are cautious, even somewhat timid entities, not driven by the same urgencies as city government. And now, from the other side of the fence, I also observed how slow city government was in its administrative functioning, as well as how slow the city was to pay its bills.

Selfhelp was my first exposure to Big Nurse, a term I use to describe the formidable powers wielded by administrative nurses responsible for upholding city and state regulations. Big Nurse has the last word on all medical and health-related issues, and if you try to argue, Big Nurse brandishes her nursing license, refusing to yield to mere civilians. When the issue arose of having health aides assist patients with administering their medication, Big Nurse was against it: *Okay for the maid but not the aide* was the phrase we used to characterize Big Nurse's insistence that only family or a nonprofessional maid could help a patient with medications ... but certainly *not* Selfhelp's trained home-care aides. On the face of it, this made no sense, but the real issue at hand was insurance liability.

In all my years in government I never thought about cash flow. In government, the holy grail had been the budget and how much I could spend. Cash flow belonged to the mayor, the governor, and the comptroller: *they* paid the bills, *they* met the payroll, *they* borrowed money. At Selfhelp, I quickly learned what business people know intuitively: that an organization lives and dies on cash flow. For a government refugee like me, this was an important lesson, and in no time I became a cash-flow hawk.

In 1995 the government of Buenos Aires invited me to speak at a conference in Argentina about home care. I hadn't realized that many

German Jewish refugees who had managed to survive the Holocaust had fled to Buenos Aires, and I learned that many of my board members had relatives and acquaintances there. So, with the blessing of their introduction, I visited our board members' family and friends in Argentina. Exactly like those who had founded Selfhelp in New York, the immigrant Argentinians had also founded organizations to help WWII refugees, as well as many others. In fact, meeting them was quite an eerie experience.... It was exactly like a Selfhelp board meeting. The men were all over 60; everyone spoke impeccable English (and Spanish) with a German accent. And, too, they had precisely the same outlook and philosophy as their counterparts in New York: be understated and polite, stay friendly with government, keep your head down, and don't make waves. Even their names were the same: Hans, Gregor, Erik, Fredrik. I later learned that my board members in Selfhelp had waited three years to even inquire as to whether I was Jewish, a question that would never have been put on hold by the Central European Jews of my own community.

While at Selfhelp, I was recruited for other executive jobs. One was as commissioner for the newly created Department of Homeless Services under Mayor David Dinkins. But only one job—HRA commissioner in the Giuliani administration—whetted my appetite even slightly. And that would have been a bad fit, given that Giuliani's anti-welfare stance was in direct opposition to mine. In the end, I stayed at Selfhelp for almost 10 years.

When Richard Aronson retired from Selfhelp and the executive director position became available, I was so disappointed when I wasn't offered the job, I went to see John Ruskay, executive director at United Jewish Appeal, an organization closely affiliated with Selfhelp. Ruskay told me point blank why I didn't get it: "It was the suits," he said, meaning that the predominantly male German Jewish board members simply couldn't see their way to hiring a woman executive director. In 30 years of a professional career, I had never been so directly victimized by chauvinism, and I was outraged. But Ruskay also informed me that an organization called Women In Need (WIN) was seeking a new CEO. Truly, when one door closes, another opens. In the end, not getting the directorship of Selfhelp opened the door to a far more challenging and rewarding position at Women In Need, where I would stay for 15½ years and from which I'd retire in December of 2015.

CHAPTER 6

WIN

IN 2000, I WAS HIRED as president and CEO of Women In Need, a small but innovative nonprofit organization that sheltered homeless families and helped them get back on their feet. WIN had been founded in 1983 by Rita Zimmer, a passionate advocate for substance-abuse treatment and services for impoverished women. A small group of WIN's volunteer board members would visit the family welfare hotels on 34th Street and offer children summer activities to relieve them of the squalor of those notorious city residences. In the 1990s, when the city gave nonprofits the option to shelter families themselves, WIN established six small family shelters featuring programs for domestic abuse and child care. It also opened two substance-abuse clinics exclusively for women. With a staff of 125 and an annual budget of just under $8 million, the organization struggled without working capital or any financial reserves. Nevertheless, WIN had a devoted board of directors and a dedicated, enthusiastic staff.

WIN's great strength was its impressive board of directors, which attracted some of the most influential women in New York. By the time I arrived, there was Susan Rudin, wife of real estate mogul Jack Rudin; Joan Weill, wife of Citigroup's Sandy Weill; and Katherine Farley, who was married to mega-developer Jerry Speyer, of Tishman Speyer. All three women were extraordinarily wealthy. Completely devoted to the cause of homeless women and children, they were also concerned that the organization could not survive. There were chronic urgent requests from Rita Zimmer for emergency cash just to meet the modest payroll.

In my first few weeks as CEO, I called vice chair Susan Rudin at her beach house. A gruff man answered the phone and asked, "Who is this?"

"I'm Bonnie Stone, the new president of WIN. May I speak with Susan?"

Oh, you're the new girl. Well, Susan is in the shower, but let me tell you something, you better not fuck this up. Susan loves this organization. I was speaking with Jack Rudin, of course, and gruff as he sounded, I knew he was a truly stellar New Yorker. He was head of a legendary real estate empire, and he and his family were among the most philanthropic, civic-minded people in town.

When the board informed me that there was a serious problem with WIN's finances, I scrutinized the daily financials. I saw that the organization was sound, but that there were serious cash-flow issues. Much of WIN's cash came from annual donations that arrived late in the fiscal year, making day-to-day operations run too close to the bone. I prepared a clear analysis and explained my findings to the board: yes, the annual budget was balanced, but city contracts that advanced money to WIN in the beginning of the fiscal year left the organization short of funds at year's end. However, generally enough money was raised from donations to fulfill annual budget requirements by the second half of the year. Nevertheless, we were always behind in terms of cash flow.

After explaining this to the board, I called Mary McCormack, president of the Fund for the City of New York, to see if she could help. I knew McCormack from city government. She was legendary, and the Fund was a highly respected foundation designed to help government and not-for-profit social service agencies. It took Mary a nanosecond to say that she'd do whatever she could.

I went to see her with board chair Katherine Farley. McCormack's first words to Farley: *Do you know how lucky you are to have Bonnie at the helm of WIN?*—a great way to start a meeting. I described our immediate cash-flow problems and explained that we needed a noncollateralized $500,000 cash-flow loan, a very big ask. McCormack listened and without much discussion simply said yes. Apparently, my track record was collateral enough. With that settled, McCormack wanted to discuss citywide homeless policy, while Farley tried to steer the conversation back to the terms of the loan. Coming from the cutthroat world of commercial real estate, Farley had a hard time believing the $500,000 was a done deal, but it was. We'd solved WIN's cash flow for the year and could move ahead to other issues. Farley was pleasantly stunned. We'd solved a critical problem, and I had passed my first test.

To establish myself at WIN, I knew I needed someone I could trust as my gatekeeper and brought on Hy Burton, a colleague from HRA and Selfhelp, who'd worked on homeless and other programs for more than 30 years. An African American from Virginia, he had come to New York for his first job as a caseworker at the old Welfare Department. Later, at HRA, Hy had been so competent and reliable he'd risen to the level of assistant commissioner. A formal yet ebullient character, Hy used to proclaim that he had so much fun working, he was amazed they even bothered to pay him. He was too young to retire, but retire he did, and moved to Miami, where he was quickly bored to death. It wasn't hard for me to coax him back to New York with a position as a social worker at Selfhelp. Now, at WIN, he'd be my executive assistant.

What made Hy Burton extremely special, if not unique, was his sense of humanity. In his first two weeks at WIN, I thought I'd lose him because he missed the "old ladies" he'd worked with at Selfhelp. But he stayed with me, and soon everyone at WIN relied on Mr. Burton for consistency and stability. Staff, skeptical board members, and the public appreciated his calm voice, commanding and thorough, directing the traffic in my office. Hy was suave and sounded a bit like Walter Cronkite. When people who called were angry or complaining, his soothing voice, his ever-professional and courteous manner, calmed them. Mr. Burton was my secret weapon.

Hy Burton had a huge heart and adopted and supported several struggling families, first in the Caribbean, then in Morocco and Thailand. On vacation in Tangiers, he met a young man working for a store in the Casbah who sold him a few pairs of socks. When he and the young man went to pay for the socks, the owner jacked up the price. When the young salesman protested, the owner backed down. The next day, Hy returned to the store, only to learn that the boy had been fired for being too honest. Hy looked around, discovered Hicham in a nearby shop, and gave him a very large tip, which marked the beginning of a long friendship. In fact, they became so close that Hy purchased a home for the young man and his family. Later, Hy even adopted him and to this day dotes on Hicham like a father. Eventually, Hicham married, and Hy is now grandfather to three small children, all of whom adore him.

Years later, on another vacation, Hy met another young man in Bangkok. Hy also "adopted" Ton and helped him make his way and succeed in the travel industry. Hy retired in 2016, not long after I did. He actually wanted to continue working but wouldn't work for anyone else. Mr. Burton still visits Morocco and Bangkok and faithfully supports his adopted families.

Robin White, another colleague from Selfhelp, joined me at WIN. Robin had actually been recruited to head the Development Department a few weeks before I was even interviewed, but while she was interested in the organization, she was very concerned about who WIN would select as their new CEO. When she learned it would be me, she immediately accepted the job.

The first year was difficult. There were hard feelings about the controversial departure of founder Rita Zimmer, a charismatic individual and a true believer in the transformative power of social services. The board had become concerned about Rita's ability to both manage the organization administratively *and* keep it financially stable. About a half dozen board members had resigned in protest, and morale was low.

WIN's actual programs for homeless women and children were quite sound and required only slight adjustments, but it didn't take me long to recognize that the organization was way too top heavy, with 25 percent of its budget devoted to administrative staff. The best solution for this imbalance was to maintain existing administrative staff while simultaneously expanding WIN's services and capacities to care for a substantially larger number of homeless families. I thoroughly analyzed WIN's finances to better understand the ebb and flow of their $8 million annual budget, including their government contracts and fundraising. Clearly, the organization had "good bones." It had a great mission and no history of corruption or scandal.

We needed to attract new board members, and I met privately with each of the 22 remaining members, all of whom had just weathered a wrenching turnover. While some board members were among the elite movers and shakers of New York, I was surprised at how pessimistic they were. "Why would anyone want to join this board?" a few asked. Still, they rolled up their sleeves and strategized an effective recruitment effort. We met monthly to consider new candidates. WIN had just mounted its first reasonably successful fundraising gala at the Cathedral of St. John the Divine and was revved up to organize the next one. Robin White spearheaded the new gala initiative, and the board began to seriously admire and respect her savvy and expertise. Private donations were critical, but we needed more leverage for real money to ensure growth. And that would come from partnering with government.

WIN's premier private funder was the not-for-profit Robin Hood Foundation, which warned me that they would cut their substantial grant in half unless I hired a viable finance person. They told me that in general, new CEOs following founders usually lasted about 18 months, and therefore they'd be watching me. Without a doubt, WIN's finance department was weak. A temporary director had been filling in, so hiring a strong, permanent Finance VP became my first priority, and I hired Irene Robling, whom I knew from her fine reputation at HRA.

I then set out to get the board comfortable with the idea of growth. They believed they couldn't do any better with fundraising than they already had, but I explained to them that true growth didn't depend on fundraising from their or anyone else's pockets, but on government contracts and grants. I worked hard to make them understand this logic, but they were not entirely ready to trust me. So, I paced myself. I slowed down but moved ahead. I contacted Ken Murphy, whom I'd known at HRA. Ken had left city government as a deputy commissioner and was currently consulting with various private landlords to develop shelters. He was doing well and, when I asked, agreed to bring me any new deals. But even before he brought in the first one, I got a call from an existing shelter looking for a new social services provider. Henry Street Settlement had terminated its subcontract with Hope Community, a not-for-profit housing agency in East Harlem. It was the perfect opportunity, the perfect first expansion for the board to digest.

The community agency would continue to administer the contract, and WIN's role would be to staff social services. Our cost would be reimbursed through the city contract. That shelter, on East 100th Street in Manhattan, was known as Jennie A. Clarke (Jennie Clarke was a revered Evangelical minister in East Harlem) and could house 73 families, each in their own apartment. It was twice as big as any of WIN's existing shelters but was still of relatively modest size, *and* this would be a partnership. The board was pleased and in no time started organizing volunteer opportunities—birthday parties and tutoring—for the 200 kids who lived there, and for their parents, résumé writing, computer training, and general education.

One extraordinary WIN VP, our VP of Client Services, who had weathered the transition from Rita to me, was Ophelia Smith. Born in North Carolina, Ophelia had a degree in German from Oberlin College and a PhD in psychology from Columbia University. She was also an accomplished pianist, having studied music in Paris for two years. Both of her parents were schoolteachers, and as an African American woman in the 1960s, Ophelia couldn't wait to get to New York, free of the constrictions of the South. We hit it off immediately, and I called Ophelia my partner in crime as we strategized the unstoppable growth of WIN. In 12 years, WIN would increase the number of people served and the number of beds for homeless families tenfold. We went from serving 450 people every night to serving 4,500 every night, most of them children. Soon, WIN served 10 percent of all the homeless families in New York City, and by the time I retired in 2015, the budget had grown from $8 million annually to $70 million.

Ophelia was the soul of WIN, quiet, dignified, and fiercely competitive. For those who worked for her, being called to her office was like being called to the principal's office in high school. If you were not performing, she'd guide you to the exit. If you were salvageable, she'd help you shape up. When she returned from an executive coaching program in South Dakota, she was all fired up to fulfill her "bucket list," a *long* one. Much of it had to do with her work at WIN, but there were plenty of personal goals, all of which she realized. She climbed in the Himalayas, renovated her kitchen, got a face-lift, lost 50 pounds, bought a baby grand, and took lessons in jazz piano. But in 2013, Ophelia was diagnosed with liver cancer and died in three months, at age 67. As she was dying, she took her vows as a Buddhist monk. Her death was a blow to the entire community. We truly loved each other, and I think about her often. After Ophelia's death, I organized a memorial at a church on Ninth Avenue. It was filled with more than a hundred people, and because Ophelia had so encouraged me, I played my guitar at the service. People were stunned.

Because I worked for the city when the homeless crisis began in the late 1970s, I understood the field. I knew what the system needed and how WIN could play an important role in improving it. Ken Murphy was now consulting with various landlords to create new shelters. I told him that WIN was ready to take on whatever he could offer. We went to work, and WIN began opening larger shelters. When I arrived, there were only six small ones, but after the success of Jennie Clarke, the board became more confident in my theory of expansion. WIN closed all but one of its original shelters; the remaining one was converted into a shelter for single women, and the rest were handed off to other organizations. In their stead, WIN opened 10 shelters that housed a total of 1,200 families. We accomplished everything with the exact same administrative staff I'd inherited, bringing on new people only after our services had tripled.

The Noble Drew Ali housing was a failed federally funded housing complex in the Brownsville neighborhood of Brooklyn. The project consisted of five large apartment buildings set around an inner courtyard. The finances were terrible, the physical plant was full of problems, and crime was rampant. Many apartments were vacant, so it was a bazaar for illegal drugs. An Orthodox Jewish developer was leasing the two worst buildings, and Ken Murphy requested that WIN take it on as a shelter. The developer had renovated the apartments, but almost immediately local politics took over and we found ourselves in the middle of a fracas involving tenants in the remaining three buildings, as well as the Housing Preservation Department (HPD), community organizers, the Reverend Louis Farrakhan (a relative of the famous Louis Farrakhan), the New York state attorney, the courts, WBAI radio, the Legal Aid Society, and local gangs. The police were reluctant to even enter the courtyard. A four-year-old was killed while he sat in his father's lap in a car parked just outside. The father, who was not living with the family, had returned for a visit. I attended the child's funeral. At one point, the reporter Jimmy Breslin came by, but he ultimately did not write about this very sad story.

The building complex had been crumbling for years, and no one wanted to deal with it. But once a private developer entered the picture, there was the smell of new money, which inevitably attracted the interest of other players. I used to visit the site and walk straight through the perilous inner courtyard. Groups of young men hung around with pit bulls on chains. It was a bad scene, but since WIN had placed families there, I made sure I was a regular presence. I counted on the "street" seeing me as just some weird white woman who was so out of place she couldn't possibly be a threat to their local order. They kept an eye on me but stood aside and let me pass.

There were a few bitter court battles over who actually controlled the site—was it the federal government, the current landlord, WIN, or HPD? All were at a standoff. Then HPD swooped in and took charge. WIN moved its 135 families to a newly renovated shelter a few miles away. Eventually, HPD renovated the old complex and made it a viable housing project.

Opening shelters in a city both dependent on and hostile to real estate development made for endless headaches, but New York City was bound by the consent decree of 1981 and compelled to face the crisis of homelessness every single day. The Human Resources Administration housed the homeless by appropriating surplus school buildings, former hospitals, armories owned by the state Guard, and so on. In 1992, when the city relinquished direct administration of shelters and gave administrative contracts to not-for-profits, the contracts included funds for leasing new properties (at prices the city itself had negotiated), resulting in even larger contracts with yet more not-for-profits. The not-for-profit would then pay the landlord based on a lease between the landlord and the not-for-profit. This provided more immediate shelter for homeless families by circumventing the city's elaborate contract process.

Most real estate developers were unfamiliar with these dynamics and wanted guarantees before they would renovate a building for shelter use. But some, in particular real estate companies from the Orthodox Jewish community, did understand shelter payment dynamics and did not demand guarantees. They spent millions renovating buildings on speculation for shelters. They gambled and ultimately made a great deal of money.

I had left HRA in 1986, before the mayoral term of David Dinkins and the first five years of the Giuliani administration. When I first came to WIN, Rudy Giuliani was still mayor. He was no friend to the homeless, but he, too, was bound by the consent decree. Try as he might, Giuliani could not arrest the growth of homelessness. He may have stopped the "squeegee" men from annoying drivers, he may even have reduced violent crime, but the tide of homelessness only grew stronger.

I began familiarizing myself with the various members of the Giuliani administration and their philosophies. I understood the city's finances and operations, and guided WIN through the maze. My experience enabled me to put deals together, and by the time I retired, WIN's staff had blossomed from 125 to more than 500 employees, and the number of homeless served nightly increased to over 4,500, including 2,600 children. WIN became the finest and largest provider of homeless family services in the city, serving 10 percent of its homeless families.

The causes of family homelessness differed from those for single men and women. Eviction and domestic violence are the biggest precursors to family homelessness, but mental illness and addiction are also factors. Usually, families enter a shelter after "couch-surfing," moving around, exhausting help from family and friends after spending, on average, a year or so doubling up. When couch-surfing runs its course, families apply for help. Their first stop is PATH, the city's intake center, on 151st Street in the Bronx. The staff at PATH determine whether the family is indeed homeless and then assign them to a shelter—hopefully close to their old neighborhood, but more often, wherever there's room at the inn. Shelters provide modest private spaces, usually with a bathroom and kitchen facilities so they can cook and maintain some semblance of family life. Children are immediately placed in school again, but the whole experience is profoundly traumatic. Teenagers, in particular, are deeply ashamed of being in a shelter and often lie about where they live. There were hundreds of stories at WIN . . . of drug abuse, domestic violence, broken families, chronic eviction. But WIN offered families hope and the opportunity for a new start.

Dina was a difficult child. As a youth she joined a gang, the Latin Kings. When she was jumped and beaten by 15 other girls, her mother sent her home to the Dominican Republic, where she thrived. Dina graduated from high school but returned to New York when her mother became ill. Back in New York, Dina worked for a while, then got pregnant. But shortly after the child was born, her boyfriend threw her out and she went to stay with her grandmother. She lived with her grandmother and five other people for a few years before entering the shelter system. Dina was assigned to two different shelters before entering a WIN shelter, where, because of WIN's various programs, she was able to begin restoring her life.

At WIN, Dina realized her son was safe; she slowly regained confidence in herself, and when she earned a certificate to work as a home health aide, she was back on track. Her day began at 6:30 in the morning. After getting her son off to school, she took two buses to her morning patient in the Bronx. In the afternoon, she traveled to her second patient. At 8:30 p.m., Dina started the long journey back to the shelter, getting home around 10, when her son had already had his dinner and gone to sleep. WIN helped Dina with child care, fostered her participation in various training programs, and in the summer, sent her son to Camp WIN, a day camp on the premises. She attended WIN-sponsored job fairs and was provided with clothing appropriate for job interviews. Eventually, Dina became a practical nurse, and she and her son moved to their own apartment. Her son grew up and attended college.

Margaret entered the shelter with four children. Her life had been one of constant domestic violence, and while she had had a good job as a nurse, she started using drugs and eventually became homeless. Tammy, a WIN counselor, met Margaret when she first arrived. Like most people who land in a shelter for the first time, Margaret had a blank stare. Her children were frightened and confused, Margaret trusted no one, and they all expected the worst. In time, Margaret took advantage of all of WIN's services, but it was her case manager, Tammy, who supported and guided her, encouraging her through all her lingering doubts. WIN helped Margaret find an apartment, and she said, "WIN helped me get control of my life. WIN gave me wings." When the moving van arrived, she said, "It felt unreal to have a key, a home, a future. It was like a fairy tale."

In 2004 Shantee, 22, and her 5-year-old daughter, Keyana, fled the home of Shantee's abusive husband at three in the morning. When the 5-year-old pointed a knife at her father and screamed, "Don't hurt my mother!" Shantee knew it was time to go. They made their way to the PATH office in the Bronx, were assigned to a shelter—at first not a WIN shelter—and their long journey began. Shantee found work but still could not begin to afford an apartment. After a year or so, the city gave Shantee a "special local voucher" for a subsidized apartment in Far Rockaway, a city/state housing subsidy issued to qualified families. With it, a family could rent an apartment by paying only 30 percent of their income toward rent, with city and state governments making up the difference. It was similar to the federal Section 8 subsidy housing. When a family's income increases, they pay 30 percent of their new income level, just as they do with federal subsidies.

Life was looking up for Shantee and her daughter when, in a budgetary struggle and fit of pure meanness, Mayor Bloomberg and Governor Andrew Cuomo came to egotistical loggerheads and precipitously ended the very successful and massively helpful local rental voucher program. It was a tragedy for thousands of previously homeless families who, for a while, tried to pay the market-rate rent, but inevitably failed. After a few months of struggling, Shantee and her daughter were evicted. For a while they stayed with friends, but after a few months they were once again homeless. This time, fortunately, PATH assigned them to WIN's Jennie A. Clarke shelter in Upper Manhattan, where they took advantage of every program.

After a year at Jennie Clarke, Shantee was working and thriving, and Keyana was growing up. WIN helped them find an apartment using federal subsidies in the Bronx, where they were finally homeless no more. Seven years later, when Shantee was 34 and Keyana 17, they returned to WIN to tell a huge audience of fundraisers and supporters that they would both be graduating in June 2018—Keyana from high school, Shantee from college. And Keyana would be attending college. The success of this single WIN family has been replicated all over the city, but the public is rarely aware of these remarkable stories of diligence and ultimate success.

One day, a young man named Robert LoCasio visited me at WIN. LoCasio had made a fortune in the tech boom. He wanted to give back and proposed donating turkeys to homeless families at Thanksgiving. Apparently, he'd approached several other not-for-profits that did not have the administrative resources to accept his offer, but WIN arranged for him to distribute turkeys at our Jennie Clarke shelter, and LoCasio personally knocked on each door, handing out turkeys. The following year, he galvanized his staff and added all the trimmings. That year, he distributed 250 Thanksgiving dinners in several shelters, and the following year, he donated complete Thanksgiving dinners to all of WIN's 1,200 families. This kind of generosity happened many times, and WIN accommodated gifts of everything from birthday parties to haircuts to craft sessions and special performances.

Fundraising was a vital part of WIN's existence. While 85 to 90 percent of funding came from government contracts for shelter operations, private money enabled the organization to upgrade and innovate services for homeless families. And it was that extra something that earned WIN the reputation of being one of the city's best and most effective providers.

Robin White, our vice president of Development, had spent much of her career in commercial branding before working with me at Self-help. At WIN, Robin became our star fundraiser in tandem with a dedicated board of directors and others in the philanthropic community. We raised a million dollars at our first annual gala in 2001 and, by the time I left, were raising between $2.5 million and $3 million a year. Most galas took place in the Waldorf Astoria ballroom and made it to the pages of the *New York Times* Style section, adding visibility and prestige and helping us attract major corporate support.

In 2003, WIN designed and carried out a capital plan to augment its cash reserves. We established a $3 million reserve fund for rainy days or to bolster cash flow when necessary. Those of us who ran day-to-day operations were scrupulously careful to leave the reserve untouched unless the board approved a special use. The system worked well, but it was also clear that we needed to focus conscientiously on increasing our cash reserve.

WIN had one substantial asset that could strengthen its finances: real estate. We owned a large brownstone on West 51st Street in Manhattan that was used as a small family shelter. The mortgage was paid, and the last three long-term single-room-occupancy (SRO) tenants had moved on. The brownstone was never really meant to be a multiple-family residence, its 30 sheltered families sharing very cramped quarters with no real privacy. In 2008 we asked the city to pay us rent for the building's use as a family shelter, figuring we could at least start to earn some income from it. The city had reimbursed us for the original mortgages, but they'd stopped when the mortgages had been satisfied. They went back and forth on our proposal but were afraid of setting a precedent, since there were other buildings around town with similar cash needs and they didn't want to have to start paying rent on all of them.

Then WIN decided to put the building up for sale. One of our board members, Laura Pomerantz, a well-known real estate professional, helped organize the sale, and soon we were receiving bids. But when we entered the tortured world of New York real estate, we discovered some incredibly problematic constraints on the sale. In an effort to preserve SRO units for low-income New Yorkers, the city had designated the Clinton neighborhood as a special zoning region. In order to sell the building, WIN had to prove that in the building's entire history, no prior SRO tenants had been harassed—even before WIN owned it. Nine months of arduous research cleared that hurdle.

Then we transferred 51st Street families to our other shelters. We accepted a bid for the sale, but just prior to closing, the bidder pulled out. The next bidder had financial problems but, while they were gathering their resources, offered to rent the building from us for use as a hostel for young, single tourists. The arrangement would be temporary, but WIN entered a war zone. Housing advocates on the West Side of Manhattan had been battling landlords for years to prevent them from selling buildings that were used as SROs to buyers who intended to transform them into tourist hostels or hotels. Advocates were vehement that this was an assault on the ever-diminishing SROs for the local homeless—which, in fact, it was. Decades before, HRA deputy administrator Robert Jorgen had warned that the SRO housing supply for low-income and homeless individuals was disappearing, and repeatedly urged the city to try to prevent the loss. But the city hadn't heeded his warning, and now a new mayoral task force for preserving SROs came after us with a vengeance.

Although we had passed the earlier city SRO nonharassment judgment in order to get the building certified for sale, the task force objected to the use of the building as a youth hostel and characterized WIN, which was entirely dedicated to housing and assisting homeless families, as an evil landlord. The task force threw the book at us. Eventually, we found a buyer who wanted to renovate the building as a shelter for single women, a proposal the community supported. Finally, it was sold for $4 million, which was immediately applied to our reserve fund and which vastly enriched our long-term fiscal health. And we negotiated with the new owner to operate the renovated shelter under a city contract. Ironically, in the end, the city finally paid a steeper rent than it would have years before, when it refused to pay us a fair one.

A critical factor in running a successful not-for-profit is management of complex finances. In my 15 years at WIN, I hired three

finance chiefs. The first, Irene Robling, had serious experience working for the HRA, which I knew would be a terrific asset. Irene had
a fine reputation, and she was a smart, independent thinker and
self-starter devoted to WIN's mission. With Irene as VP of Finance,
I felt secure and was able to concentrate on WIN's expansion and
growth. After seven years, Irene left to take a less arduous position
so that she could devote more time to her family.

After Irene, I hired a woman who looked good on paper, someone
with an advanced degree from the University of Chicago and a series
of impressive consulting jobs. But within weeks I realized that she
was totally incapable. When she told me we would be bankrupt in
six months, I knew I had made a serious mistake. Her prediction
was absurd, and when I tried to show her how she had misread the
data, she was obdurate. She had already begun to frighten the new
board treasurer. Even with my thorough explanations of why this
wasn't true, the senior board members were confused, uneasy, and
very concerned. Also, I had to conduct myself carefully, since the
assessments of the finance officer carried so much weight.

When WIN's board held a meeting with her to discuss the "situation," her presentation only demonstrated a total lack of understanding. The board was surprised by her cluelessness, and I was able to
fire her. One of my staff members used to say that she could make
the coffee nervous. I was relieved to see her go, but my reputation
had been damaged and I had to restore the board's confidence in me.

To find a new finance officer, we created a screening committee
and hired an executive recruiter. We interviewed some very impressive people and finally hired Eric Rosenbaum, an expert in financial
analysis and logistics from the private sector. Eric also had advanced
degrees, and he was especially pleased to be able to put his shoulder
to the wheel of WIN's mission. He systematized and computerized
finances and quickly gained my confidence as well as that of the
board. And because his talents were broader than just finance, after
several years, I engaged him in managing basic shelter operations
such as maintenance and security. Eric's computerization of those
operations was critical, since WIN was now a large organization
with more than 500 employees.

In 2012, Hurricane Sandy slammed New York City. Lower Manhattan was inundated. The Rockaways were flooded, and on Staten
Island, thousands were suddenly homeless. New York's Emergency
Services and the Red Cross opened temporary shelters. At home one
night I received a call from the deputy commissioner for Homeless
Services: "Could you open a family shelter for Sandy victims in the
next two days?" I answered yes, knowing full well how nearly impossible that would be. But emergency focuses the mind, and the WIN
staff and the city worked together on a plan. The city owned a building in the Bronx that had been unoccupied for two years and could
be reopened quickly. We would reestablish water and heat, and an
existing city contract would enable us to deliver food. The city would
provide beds, chairs, etc. WIN would supply staffing, sheets, and
blankets as well as other necessities and manage the facility. Months
later, the city utilized an emergency contract to pay us back for a substantial cash outlay. But this was a real emergency, and I knew that
even if it took time, the city would honor its promise.

I got another call the next morning at work from the same deputy
commissioner: "Can you open that Bronx shelter tonight instead of
tomorrow? We really need the beds." I groaned, but agreed. That day
was a mad dash, and staff rushed to the Bronx to get things ready
pronto. At 5 p.m., buses began arriving with the first bedraggled
families. We sheltered families and individuals as well as pets of all
types—dogs, cats, birds . . . even snakes. Angela Gonzalez, a WIN
VP, was managing the site and called me later that evening: "We
have a family here with two big, muzzled pit bulls. What should I do
with them?" "Take them in," I answered. "But make sure the muzzles
stay on!"

The shelter was not a pretty sight, but this was an emergency, and
for these displaced New Yorkers, it was a warm, dry place to stay. I
was so proud of our staff for their flexibility and enthusiasm. Like all
New Yorkers, they loved being a part of the solution in an emergency.
That first day, the city informed us that dinner was on its way, but at
6:30 there was still no food. WIN bought 80 pizzas for dinner. The
city promised breakfast the following morning, and that did arrive.

The shelter operated for several months as the city worked to place people. Sandy was an enormous disaster, but WIN's board and staff were proud, even exhilarated, to have been able to help. Eventually, everyone displaced by the hurricane was relocated, but soon the city requested that we reopen that same Bronx shelter for the general homeless population, whose numbers were only increasing.

WIN had become a very large, very responsible agency, and its major pillar and support was its board of directors. Over 15 years, I worked with four sensational board chairs, each of whom possessed unique strengths. Katherine Farley, who had hired me, shouldered the heavy lift of the very delicate transition from WIN's founder to me. She put her velvet gloves and steel grip to good use. Farley is a prominent architect and businesswoman who later chaired the board at Lincoln Center.

WIN's vice chair, Judy Loeb Goldfein, assumed the chair when Katherine stepped down. Judy was the New York director of Emily's List and knew everything about fundraising's peaks and valleys. She launched WIN's first successful capital campaign.

The recession of 2008 hit us especially hard, and we had to make severe cutbacks. A relatively new board member, Charlotte Prince, succeeded Judy, and Charlotte helped us navigate very stormy financial times. She maintained a sure, steady hand that kept both the board and the organization on an even keel so that WIN never experienced the internal strife that usually accompanies serious money troubles. And whatever losses we incurred, we recovered within three years.

After Charlotte's tenure, Jaqui Lividini became chair and introduced WIN to the inevitable world of marketing and public relations. Fundraising had become more competitive, and Jaqui worked hard to brand WIN as a nonprofit worthy of broad support. And, as a former VP of Saks Fifth Avenue, Jaqui of course had great style, which rubbed off on everybody.

Full board meetings and countless committee meetings during my tenure at WIN were remarkably disciplined, constructive, and civil. The 35-member board was composed of all women, and even the most challenging topics were resolved in reasonable consensus. In my 15 years, there was only one split vote, and that one was political. When Mayor Bloomberg was attempting to run for a third term, he wanted all the city's contract agencies to write letters of support. One faction of the board stressed that WIN was a nonprofit, so it shouldn't enter the political fray. The vote was split. In the end, the issue fizzled out when the mayor's office withdrew the request.

Meanwhile, WIN had become an indispensable player in the city's response to homelessness. After 15 years at WIN, I decided to retire. New leadership would map out WIN's future, and after a national search, the board selected Christine Quinn, who'd served as New York City Council Speaker for eight years, as WIN's new president and CEO.

CHAPTER 7

STONE HOUSE

IN 2006, JOEL SHAFRAN AND I stood on Junius Street in Brooklyn looking at an almost abandoned block adjacent to two of WIN's largest shelters. Those shelters—Junius and Liberty—housed a total of 419 homeless families, about 1,500 people in all, including 1,000 children. And Joel was the commercial owner of both. He was one of WIN's most prized partners in providing quality shelter. Joel is a prince, a man of his word, and a risk taker with a big heart. We trusted each other. In our business he was a dream landlord who never sweated the small stuff and who helped out whenever he could. He made a lot of money, but he gave back too.

Joel wanted to build another shelter on the nearly abandoned lot, but it was clear that neither WIN nor the city believed that another large shelter right beside two others would be a very good idea. Then Joel and I began to explore the idea of permanent housing on the site. Permanent housing would be a huge learning curve, but we were game and started out on the long and difficult journey to try to make it happen. Joel completely understood that he would not make the same kind of money that leasing shelter buildings earned; still he was interested in learning about the intricacies of government-supported permanent housing. We agreed that he would lay out all the predevelopment money and the bureaucratic work would be my responsibility. We shook hands on it, and almost immediately, Joel purchased the site. Our board accepted the challenge when I assured them that none of WIN's savings would be used.

In fact, without a single legal commitment, we spent the next 10 years doing what you had to do in the city of New York to build government-supported housing: coming up with the design, holding community consultations, obtaining approval for a zoning change from the Board of Standards and Appeals, attending public hearings, writing partnership papers, and seeking public financing. When all this had been accomplished, it then took 2½ years to construct what would become the largest supported housing project in the city. Along the way there were stop signs, pitfalls, barricades, and detours aplenty. The project had at least five near-death experiences, but each time we persevered and worked through until we got what we needed.

Joel's partners felt the project was not worth the trouble, and WIN allowed me to continue mostly because WIN was not committing any of its own money. Nevertheless, Joel's and my goal of providing what would become 160 apartments for formerly homeless families and other low-income New Yorkers kept us focused.

We had assembled what we thought was a dream development team. We brought on building finance specialist Amy Larovere and Tony Shitemi, an experienced architect well known to the city. Our attorneys were Allen Epstein, an expert in subsidized housing, and WIN's own pro bono attorney from the Willkie Farr law firm. When Allen died in 2013, his colleague, Oliver Chase, stepped up.

Our first meeting with the city's Housing Preservation and Development Agency was not encouraging. In fact, we were practically thrown out of the room. HPD had not worked with us in the past and we had no track record with them, *and* the model we were suggesting didn't fit into their plans. Till then, they'd only dealt with city-owned land and housing for single homeless people. Our plan involved private land, homeless families with children, and a partnership with the private sector. What I did not realize until I recently told the story to a former HPD commissioner, Paul Crotty, was that HPD was obsessed with staying away from anything that came close to homelessness. Yes, their mission was to build housing, but they, like many others, believed the homeless were a curse that would frighten communities and make their projects unpalatable.

WIN was devoted to homeless people and services, and so, even though our project was for permanent supportive housing, HPD perceived any hint of association with the homeless as dangerous. Their attitude put a damper on our initiative and helped delay the project for years.

The site required a zoning change from manufacturing to residential, so we outlined our plan with the city's Bureau of Standards and Appeals (BSA) to see if the change was possible. When they informally gave us the green light, our next stop was Community Board #16, where we made a high-level presentation to their very skeptical land-use committee. To our surprise, they liked the plan and even applauded our presentation. But when we were called back for a second meeting, the atmosphere completely changed. We were criticized for not having first presented to the East New York Development Corporation (ENYDC), the local development organization. The Community Board was concerned about the zoning change and the site's proximity to a large junkyard, the Long Island Railroad freight line, and the L subway line. We agreed to address them all.

Then we had a disastrous meeting with the ENYDC, whose objections to the nearby junkyard were severe; they were concerned about the possibility that children might play there. Our next stop was the full Community Board. This time, in order to bolster the idea that we were already part of the community, we brought along about a dozen WIN staff members who actually lived in the local community. But the board chair had heard about the plan and refused to hear us out. In fact, she refused to allow us to speak at all, and only one member of the community audience stood up in support of the project. We'd walked into a firestorm. As far as we could tell, the hostility did come from some legitimate environmental concerns, but I think that deep down, the Community Board was offended at not having been involved from the very beginning. Nor could they comprehend that Joel was using his own private money to buy the land. They were going to make it difficult for us, and we'd have to win them over.

Our next step was political. We visited Brooklyn borough president Marty Markowitz. He and his staff were impressed and pledged some financial support. That was encouraging, so we revisited the Bureau of Standards and Appeals, whose original green light had turned caution yellow. Apparently, there were conflicts with the East New York industrial business district in which the site was located. We argued that the land we proposed to build on was on the other side of the railroad tracks from the bigger industrial park and that any substantial land mitigation would be too expensive for an ordinary business. The land we wanted to use was polluted from years of coal deposits and had been vacant for over 60 years. And, just to complicate matters, the community was objecting and protesting yet again. It literally took two years of hearings at the BSA and, from 2009 to 2011, additional analyses of sound and pollution.

Before the end of the hearings, I arranged for two deputy mayors, Linda Gibbs from Social Services and Robert Steel from Economic Development, to discuss the conflicting city policies this project touched on. The city had two primary interests: (*a*) retaining manufacturing jobs and (*b*) building affordable housing. Because the location we were proposing had been reserved for manufacturing, the deputy mayors needed to hash out whether this particular housing project could proceed. But because our plan included money for full land remediation, they gave us the go-ahead.

However, the recession of 2008 struck, and city government ground to a halt. Nevertheless, WIN persevered, seeking financing and making design modifications to satisfy our many critics. Finally, in 2011, the BSA gave its approval for 160 apartments with a modest retail space on the ground floor. Because the BSA had taken notice of the relatively high level of political involvement in the project, in the report describing their final decision, they enumerated all their findings at great length.

We kept working to assemble the $80 million needed for financing. Ultimately, we patched together eight different funding sources, including an unexpected $4 million grant from the Bank of America, which BofA had to spend as the result of a federal Department of Justice mortgage settlement. Other sources were two low-interest mortgages from the New York City Housing Development Corporation, a mortgage from the New York City Department of Housing Preservation and Development, a mortgage loan from the New York State Homeless Housing Assistance Corporation, a deferred developer loan from Glenmore Developers LLC, Equity Investment for low-income housing tax credits, and a grant from the Brooklyn borough president.

The most difficult negotiation was with the New York State Homeless Housing Assistance Corporation, an agency specifically charged with supporting capital projects for the homeless. They were leery of having a private partner in the mix and demanded that ownership be split 51-49, with WIN retaining controlling interest. Our partner, Joel Shafran, agreed. We also obtained a nine-year social service contract for $2 million annually from the New York City Department of Mental Health to be used to support homeless families with special needs.

In May 2015, nine years after Joel and I first discussed it and after having assembled the $80 million, we closed the deal. The closing took three full days with about a dozen people, mostly lawyers. There were endless details and last-minute changes, but the project became a reality. We were finally going to build government-supported permanent housing for 160 families comprising approximately 500 individuals. On a bright, chilly day in June 2015, we held a groundbreaking ceremony. All the naysayers who'd opposed it, as well as our numerous supporters, came together to celebrate. In the end, WIN had made good friends of all.

Joel Shafran got the apartment complex built. Always bringing a supply of delicious Danish, Joel met every week with the architect, the general contractor, project managers, expediters, an independent construction manager, and WIN staff, with all the city's regulatory agencies and financial inspectors following every step of way. The atmosphere was collegial and enthusiastic because they all loved the project. At one point, I was able to help because they needed permission from the Long Island Railroad in order to build so close to its freight tracks, and I was able to get our request prioritized by calling a few of my old LIRR colleagues.

While I joined the construction site meetings a few times to monitor progress, Joel supervised the construction. It was thrilling to

watch the building rise floor by floor. Six stories high, it was designed to look like a series of six separate buildings in order to break
the monotony of a single façade of almost 350 feet. As someone re-
marked, *This isn't a building, it's a whole neighborhood.*

After more than 15 special years leading WIN, I retired on December 31, 2015. At my farewell luncheon, the board presented
me with a photo facsimile of the finished building named Stone
House in my honor. I could hardly have been more proud. On top
of the thrill of having realized this project and of having the building named after me, Stone House was personally meaningful since
my parents, Sau and Mike, had been born and raised in the same
Brownsville neighborhood a hundred years before. For me, Stone
House was also a monument to them.

In the late summer of 2017, WIN received almost 50,000 applications from low-income families for 64 of the apartments in Stone
House, and in May 2018, they began moving in. The remaining 96
apartments had been reserved for families in the shelter system with
special needs; the apartments were especially designed for them. By
July 2018, 160 homeless families from the community and the shelter system moved into their own homes. WIN staff told me that
almost everyone who got an apartment in Stone House wept with
joy. In June, more than 100 people, including relatives, friends, and
colleagues, as well as a few new residents, attended the official ribbon
cutting for Stone House, a joyful and completely inspired ceremony.

A 39-year-old mother of two was the first resident to tell her story. She had survived a few abusive relationships, as well as a toxic
mix of bipolar disorder, depression, acute anxiety, and panic attacks.
She had been in the city's shelter system for nine years, the last six
in a WIN shelter right across the street from Stone House. Her
children, a 19-year-old girl and a 17-year-old boy, had grown up in
shelters, and as she watched the new building being constructed, she
prayed that one day she and her children might live in it. In March
2018, her dream came true.

She told the story of being shown a completely furnished apartment in advance, thinking it was a "model apartment." When they
said no, that in fact it was her actual apartment, furnishings and all,

she broke down and cried. Finally, she was able to give her son and daughter bedrooms of their own. She'd be more than happy to sleep in the living room. The kids had never before told anyone they lived in shelters for fear of being shunned or bullied, and now they could have friends over. She told the audience that now she was so happy she felt like she could accomplish anything.

When we'd visited with her earlier in the day, she'd told us how blown away she was when she discovered that her oven actually had a light in it for checking the food . . . pure luxury. She was brimming with grateful appreciation. She also told us she had had a panic attack recently, and one of WIN's counselors had rushed upstairs to her apartment and held her until her panic subsided. Happiness and hope were written all over her, but you could also see her fragility. She was exactly the person we had in mind when Stone House was created.

Epilogue

OMELESSNESS IS BOTH SIMPLE and incredibly complex. It has been with us for 40 years, and no New York City administration has been able to solve it or even slow it down, because homelessness is a tragic result of the failure to address major social and economic issues. In my view, New York City's sustained commitment to tackling homelessness is one that should be praised and not criticized. We are the only jurisdiction in the country to have made and honored a commitment to the homeless for decades, and our sustained response is the strongest in the country. Most cities do *something* in an effort to house *some* homeless, but none has made a commitment that comes even close to the dedication of New York City.

The ways in which people become homeless run the gamut from catastrophic events like a fire or eviction to the personal tragedies of domestic violence and drug and alcohol abuse. They become homeless because of the inadequacies of our education, health, and prison systems and, most critically of all, because of the almost total absence of affordable housing. Homeless people are single men and women, families with children, runaway teens . . . Some people are homeless for a few days, some are homeless for years, and some people are homeless their whole lives. There are people who issue from generations of homelessness and those who are tragically new.

Once upon a time, when people thought of city government, they thought of garbage collection, driver's licenses, and maybe snow removal. When I went to work for the city, I pretty much thought the same, and even with a master's degree in urban planning, I could easily see myself working for the Sanitation Department administrating garbage collection—doing something practical and measurable for results you could see.

In the beginning I didn't have a clue about the endless challenges and Herculean expectations of city government—of its extent, its reach. I was hired at the end of the Lindsay era, when ideals were lofty but knowing how to actually implement them . . . well, that was another story. Clearly, the Lindsay era's glamorous reach exceeded its grasp. Still, when Abe Beame succeeded John Lindsay, the contrast was profound. The combined fiscal crisis and return of the old guard was painful. The thrill was certainly gone. During the Beame administration, I witnessed a deputy mayor and a budget official actually compose the city budget on a matchbook cover. I, personally, was fortunate enough to be involved in programs that still worked to make the lives of New Yorkers better.

Not until Edward Koch was elected in 1977 did I fully comprehend the impact of good leadership at the highest levels. Koch was flamboyant, but he was also a true problem solver and a very serious student of government. He respected competence up and down the line. While there was hostility toward him from the African American community, those of us who worked with him in the trenches admired his diligence and sincerity. And of course, Ed Koch was the ever-entertaining equal-opportunity insulter of whoever disagreed with or insulted him. But he was a stand-up guy who never threw us under the bus, not even in the hottest controversies. Koch's leadership was strong and unusual. It made real change possible. My seven years working on the methadone program followed by seven years at HRA showed me what it takes to make things happen. If it doesn't last, it isn't real.

Postscript

FTER COLLEGE, when I was asked what I wanted to do, it stopped me in my tracks. *I want to do good*, I thought. I didn't know what that meant, but I knew I wasn't motivated by money or fame or, for that matter, any particular profession. I was smart but socially immature and clueless about the world. The only thing I was sure of was my home and my family. My father had no doubts about my ability, and in fact, he really wanted me to be president of the United States. That was in the 1960s, and I've since read that successful women often had fathers who totally believed in them.

Finally, I'd like to acknowledge three women who supported me through thick and thin. The first is Teena Doykos, whom I met when I started working at HRA. Teena was an old-timer, and at first she couldn't stand me. She thought I was arrogant, naïve, and inexperienced . . . and she wasn't all wrong. But after working together for a while, Teena and I respected each other and eventually became lifelong friends. She was a Greek American from Astoria, Queens, where her father had been a prominent business and community leader. When her children were grown, she accepted a "no-show" job in city government. A no-show job is a political favor position for those who worked for the Democratic party and their candidates. But nobody told Teena it was no-show, so she went to work every single day and was fantastic at managing both the subtle and broad strokes of any political situation.

Teena educated me about the world of New York City politics, and there were politics in *everything*. When we went to a meeting with Tom Cuite, Speaker of the City Council, and afterward I told Teena I hadn't understood a single word that was said, she roared with laughter and said it was all political shorthand. Teena understood it all, but it was a totally new language to me. She was respected by all the local politicos, and years later I hired her at the Long Island Railroad. I used to call Teena a witch because she could see through walls and people. Her instincts were amazing. She was a close friend until her death at age 79 in 2007.

Next is Able Rae, whom I met at Pathwork, a spiritual group I joined a couple of years after leaving government. Able was from Georgia, a writer and a storyteller with a deep southern accent. Able opened the door to a more spiritual life, and through her, I learned I had real feelings, a new sensation for me.

And, last but hardly least, my cousin Susan Weiss, an attorney and social activist. When my parents were gone, Susan opened my world to an extensive, loving family of newly discovered relatives. I never paid much attention to little Susan growing up, but as adults we've grown so close, Susan has become the sister I never had.

Acknowledgments

I'D LIKE TO ACKNOWLEDGE all the terrific people I worked with in five decades in all three levels of government, as well as in the private and nonprofit sectors. They made my career possible and have my greatest admiration and respect.

Quite a few people helped me write *Gimme Shelter*, especially my husband Jack Deacy, whose constant refrain was "Put words on paper!" When I did, he took my faltering words and edited and rewrote many passages many times.

Karen Garthe, my dear friend, picked up the final rewriting, organizing, and editing, and brought the book to fruition. Her knowledge and style added much to the final product.

I'd also like to thank Jared R. Pike, an early editor, for his invaluable encouragement, as well as former colleagues who weighed in: Robert Trobe, Kathryn Ruby, and Adrienne Leaf.

Special thanks go to Tony Shitemi, the architect who designed and built Stone House, and Joel Shafran who selflessly partnered with me on the project.

I'd also like to thank members of my family who read and commented on various drafts of *Gimme Shelter*, especially Gretchen Stone with her eagle eye.

Finally, I'd like to thank Ken Feisel, my publisher, who designed this book and its beautiful cover and brought it over the finish line.

CPSIA information can be obtained
at www.ICGtesting.com
Printed in the USA
BVHW081922061121
620943BV00005B/42/J

9 780988 267541